Eric
and the
Mystical Bear

PETER L WARD

Illustrated by STEVE CRISP

Order this book online at www.trafford.com
or email orders@trafford.com

Most Trafford titles are also available at major online book retailers.

Print information available on the last page.

ISBN: 978-1-4269-5501-3 (sc)
ISBN: 978-1-4269-5500-6 (hc)
ISBN: 978-1-4269-5502-0 (e)

Library of Congress Control Number: 2011902195

Trafford rev. 10/23/2020

www.trafford.com

North America & international
toll-free: 844-688-6899 (USA & Canada)
fax: 812 355 4082

This final part of the Viking Trilogy is dedicated to Grandson Jack

Contents

CHAPTER ONE

The Dam Across
The Stream

In a secret spot in the Saxon forest, the faint scent of fading bluebells drifted on the breeze. Soft sunlight filtered through the tops of the trees. Freya, a Viking girl who no longer lived in her homeland across the sea, lingered on the grassy path.

"The foxgloves will be out soon," she thought. "Pink bells with white spots."

She sighed, thinking fondly of the old village where her parents still lived. How she missed them. Would they ever forgive her? Freya and her friends had deserted their families to sail the land of Anglo-Saxons.

Her companion, Vimp, a tall boy with knotted strands of golden hair on his shoulders, stopped short. He had caught a glimpse of shy deer amongst the trees. Suddenly startled, they sniffed the air, looked round and turned. The white flashes of their rumps disappeared as they bolted for cover. Vimp respected wild animals.

"I'd never want to harm them," he thought. "They've got enough enemies."

The deer lived in daily fear of the hounds and spears of Saxon hunters. Vimp always avoided the chase, preferring to help the villagers build fishing boats. Stopping by a low pile of stacked logs, he spoke quietly.

"We'll turn down this track. It gets steep further on, where it's boggy. The stream's just beyond."

Freya followed him. Two cock nightingales sang noisily at each other from bushes, close by. The one singing longest and loudest hoped to attract a mate.

"We're getting close," said Vimp. "Take care. The path's slippery. Last time, I fell into the mud!"

Freya remembered laughing when her best friend returned to the village with dirty, wet marks on his rough tunic.

"Boys!" she thought. "Will they ever grow up?"

Vimp held out his hand to guide her through the swampy area. There was no path and mud squelched under their rough sandals. The two youngsters clambered over damp tree roots to reach a bend in the stream.

"Be still!" warned Vimp in a hushed tone.

In the cool air, the two young Vikings stood rigid as fragile mayflies danced over the fast current.

"Best to crouch down," he suggested. "The beavers mustn't spot us."

His eyes seemed glued to the water and Freya wondered what he had seen. Was it a fish? That was unlikely. The small stream was only good for minnows. Vimp pointed to a spot, higher up.

"D'you see?"

Freya made out a higgledy-piggledy pile of branches that blocked the course of the stream.

"They've built right across. From one side to the other."

She saw a small dam woven tightly with sticks and branches. It blocked the water flow so the level rose. It looked as though the stream, beyond, might burst its banks.

"I knew you'd want to see this in daylight," said Vimp. "We can come back tonight. That's when the beavers come out to build."

He smiled.

"They're never satisfied. Cutting new pieces and shoving them in to make their dam more water-tight."

Freya's heart raced.

"Best keep this spot a secret," she suggested. "Just between you and me."

But she swiftly changed her mind.

"I guess we should tell Lief and English Emma. Oh...and Astrid and Big Eric, of course. We musn't leave those two out. Eric gets into huffs!"

Vimp agreed.

"He can be very moody," he said. "There'll be a full moon, tonight. Why don't we all come down?"

His keen eye was caught by a thin tree stump sticking out of the swamp. It had been sawn off by something sharp and its frayed ends showed white.

"I saw a beaver gnawing that tree," he said. "It kept on doing it until the trunk snapped. Then it backed off as the tree toppled into the stream!"

It had always been Freya's hope to see beavers. In the Viking forest near their old village, she had been able to attract wild creatures to her...song birds, deer, rabbits, even wolves. Freya always felt safe in their company. However, she had never found beavers. They had been hunted almost to extinction.

The full moon rose in the starry night sky as six youngsters made their way cautiously through the wood. Vimp led, holding a lantern glowing yellow in the dark, with Big Eric at the rear. Finding their way down the shadowy path was not easy. Twice,

Vimp had to stop and turn back to find the right way. Astrid made sure she stayed near Eric who was never scared.

"We're getting close!"

Vimp passed his whispered message back to Lief who sent it down the line.

"I'll have to blow out the lantern," Vimp said. "We'll wait for a short while so our eyes can get used to the dark."

Emma, the Saxon girl, felt a cold shiver run down her spine. Long shadows reached out like extended fingers through the trees. The only sound was that of the excited breathing of her friends. In the near silence, she reached out to clutch Lief's hand. The party moved on, nearer to the stream. They heard its busy chuckle as the waters swirled around boulders and roots.

"No further!"

Vimp crouched behind a fallen trunk, rotting in the swamp. The others followed. Kneeling in cold mud was horrible and Emma wondered why she had bothered to come. The night was colder than she had imagined. She settled down into her uncomfortable, wet spot and peered over the top of the trunk. Her eyes began to adjust and it was fortunate that the moon's light fell on the swirling stream. It glistened, ever changing, as a thin ray fell on the untidy pile of branches. Freya and Vimp had spotted these earlier. Emma felt a tug on her arm. Lief detected a quick movement, just above the surface, at the base of the dam.

"Straight ahead," he whispered in her ear. "D'you see?"

He was right. Something, dark and humpy, swam through the water. Larger than she had imagined, it carried a long branch in its teeth. The whiskered animal struck out for the dam where it busied itself pushing the stick into the pile. Then it slid back into the water, flipping its paddle tail with a splash. A minute later, the beaver broke surface, again, and clambered half out of the water. With its paws, it padded mud into the dam, sealing up gaps that let the water through.

Lief tightened his grip on Emma's arm. Just beyond the growing dam sat another beaver, its tail showing beyond its wet fur. And the front paws were wrapped around a small tree. Tilting its head from side to side, the beaver slashed into the thin trunk with razor sharp teeth. The tree started to give way but the beaver stopped. It turned its head, hearing something on the wind. Even Emma, whose hearing was not as good as the beavers, could hear clumsy, clumping sounds. Was a big animal approaching the stream? The beaver stopped work and headed for the safety of the water.

Emma froze. It might be a bear. She had heard that one or two survived in this deep part of the forest. A light shone, bobbing through the trees. It grew larger, followed by a second and a third. Not bothering to hide the fact they were in the wood, a small group of Saxon boys hurried down to the stream. The beaver watchers lay still behind their fallen trunk. Flickering lights from the lanterns played over the scene, making shadows that danced into the trees.

"Right here!"

It was a rough voice. Emma recognised its owner at once; Egeslic, an unlikeable Saxon boy from the village. He seemed to have three or four others with him. Emma saw they carried stout clubs.

"Smash up the dam. Get them moving," Egeslic laughed. "If you get a chance, get in a good blow. We can make money on their skins."

Emma, an English girl amongst Viking friends, felt ashamed her own people were about to kill innocent creatures. The gang ventured nearer the dam to begin probing its outer defences. Suddenly, a loud voice boomed out of the darkness. It was a Viking voice but the language it spoke was Saxon.

"Stay where you are, Egeslic. Keep away from that dam!"

Emma stared open-eyed at the towering figure, lit in the yellow glow of the lanterns.

Eric Bignose stood brave and defiant. The Saxon boys backed off but Egeslic faced him up.

"Why, it's our Viking friends!" he jeered. "Is that ugly Eric with the long nose?"

He grinned at his companions.

"The big Viking thinks he can spoil our fun!"

There was little fun to be had. Big Eric stepped over the trunk and strode forward. He was swiftly followed by Vimp and Lief, scrambling up on their feet. The sight of angry Eric was too much for the Saxons who turned and fled, the lights of their lanterns disappearing with them. No-one, not even Egeslic, dared face the Viking boy whose reputation for courage was a legend.

"Go on. Run!" he shouted after them. "Don't ever come back here or you'll have me, Eric Bignose, to answer to!"

The three girls joined the boys. Freya was impressed.

"If we hadn't come here, tonight," she said, "those beavers would have been destroyed. Well done, Eric. And Vimp and Lief!"

The small party of beaver watchers left the stream to trudge back to their adopted village where they had been allowed to settle.

"There's going to be trouble," Vimp told the rest, grimly. "The last thing we want is to upset the Saxons. That Egeslic will make life tricky for us!"

* * * *

CHAPTER TWO

A Blooded Nose

"We found this huge tree in the forest," Vimp said. "It was perfect to make the keel of the new boat. So we cut it down and dragged it to the riverbank. But first, you have to sink it in water for a few months."

Lief looked puzzled. He was a hopeless carpenter and envied Vimp's skills. The other Viking boys also knew their stuff. But working with his hands was a mystery to Lief. His big aim in life was to learn to read and write in the language of the Anglo-Saxons. He thought back to the time when he and his friends had sailed across the sea from the land of the Vikings. After they had convinced the Saxons they were not raiders, they settled happily enough in the village. And it was the crew's skills in boat-building and that made them useful. Unfortunately, this did not apply to poor Lief.

"I'm hopeless with my hands," he confessed. "I'll stick to reading and writing this new language. It's not easy getting your head around Anglo-Saxon."

The thought saddened him. Within weeks of landing, Lief had been taken to a monastery to live with the monks, or Brothers, as they called themselves. After only a short time, the monastery had been attacked by raiders from his Viking lands. It was set on fire and valuable treasures stolen. Many of the Brothers were murdered and Lief, himself a Viking, was lucky to escape with his life.

Now he was back in the Saxon village and trying to earn a living. But not at building boats. Why, for instance, had Vimp insisted the great tree trunk, to be the boat's keel, should be soaked in salt water?

"It's the way the old Viking shipwrights were taught," his friend explained. "Soaking for months toughens the wood. We'll drag it out, soon, and get to work."

The thought horrified poor Lief who glanced at his delicate hands. Vimp laughed.

"Don't worry! We'll give you the easy jobs. Even a spot of time off to do your writing. Perhaps you'll come up with a great poem about the new boat? Alfred, the village Chieftain, might read it out at the launch!"

The two boys reached the bank of the river where the craft was to be put together. Half a dozen young Vikings wielded axes and mallets. The percussive sounds of banging and scraping hurt Lief's tender ears. Bjorne Strawhead took a break.

"Come to give us a hand, Lief?" he grinned. "We've left the heavy stuff for you."

The young poet gritted his teeth.

"I'll do my best. You know that."

The days passed and the submerged log was dragged from the river bottom. Ropes had been knotted round and the boys put their backs into tugging it back up the bank. Big Eric took charge.

"Pull!" he commanded.

Bjorne slipped over in the mud. The rest of the hauling party struggled to a halt. Eric encouraged Bjorne to get to his feet.

"Don't worry!" he called over, cheerfully. "Where are the Saxon boys? They said they'd help us. Why haven't they turned up?"

Bjorne knew the answer.

"They'll appear at any the moment," he said. "Just after we've finished dragging this thing into place. They always get out of the heavy work."

Exhausted, the small party of Vikings finally positioned the trunk on the spot where the boat would be built. Lief the poet put his slender back into the task. Once they had succeeded, he slumped down in the sun to rest. Words began to form in his mind; words worthy of the longboat that would soon set out to sail.

Alfred, the Saxon Chief, had asked the young Vikings to design and build a boat that could go out and do battle. Vimp and his friends knew the village could be raided, at any moment. Alien Vikings, thieves and plunderers, might destroy homes and carry off cattle and sheep. The people might end up as slaves. By building this big boat, Vimp and his friends could prove to the Saxons whose side they were on.

Vimp got up stiffly from the churned up ground and flexed his aching limbs. He selected an axe and ran his thumb gingerly down the blade.

"Hmm. Sharp," he thought. "Better be careful."

He picked up a second tool. This, too, had a strong handle to grip. Its metal blade had been curved over in the heat of the furnace.

"An adze," he thought. "Handy for shaping wood. This one's well made."

Just then, he heard a cheery call from the nearest hut. It was a girl's voice, loud and clear.

"Lunch for hungry boat-builders!"

The boys scrambled to their feet to find Freya, Ingrid, Astrid and English Emma walking towards the shore. Each girl carried a large, woven basket.

"Right on time!" thought Vimp. "Am I hungry?"

The girls struggled down to the riverbank.

"Wash your hands!" Astrid called out. "Just look at the state of you. Disgusting! No one's having a bite to eat until they've cleaned up."

She shot a glance at Eric.

"Especially you, Eric Bignose!" she giggled, tossing her curls. Embarrassed Eric looked sheepish and hid his large, grimy hands behind his back.

"Go on!" Astrid ordered. "Not a bite until you've cleaned up!"

The tall Viking boy wanted to be seen at his best in Astrid's company. They had shared so many adventures, together. Eric looked around at his friends as they put down their tools and sat on the grass. The tide had turned, so water streamed from the river mouth to the sea. Eric dreamt of the day the longboat would be launched but that would be weeks from now. Hours of work were still needed to cut and shape the timbers. These would be riveted together and the gaps plugged with wool and tar. Eric especially wanted to be given the job of making the rudder. By now, he had gained respect for steering his comrades across the North Sea. Strong Eric had battled storms and mountainous waves at the helm. He also seemed to understand how to navigate, taking his bearings from the position of the sun, or the stars.

The boat-builders enjoyed their short lunch break with the girls, handing out hunks of cheese and lumps of bread. There was foaming beer to drink from jugs.

"Not too much," Astrid warned. "We don't want you all falling asleep. You haven't finished, for today."

English Emma passed round juicy, red apples she had picked only that morning. She sat with Lief and asked him if he had come up with any good ideas for his new poem. He shook his head, unhappily.

"Not a thing!" he complained. "Writing isn't like boat-building. With a boat, you turn up in the morning and do your job. But when I write, I need to imagine. Perhaps I need to get away from here. All this bashing and banging does my head in!"

Emma was about to say something consoling when she looked up and saw a group of Saxon teenagers approaching. They had been picking up stones in the fields; back-breaking work to help the farmers. One or two carried sharp flints in their hands but kept them out of sight. Emma sensed the young Saxons were out for trouble. She was disturbed to see Egeslic at their head. Vimp got up on his feet and faced the bully up.

"What d'you want?" he asked. "We don't want trouble."

Egeslic, big for his age, took the lead.

"We didn't know you Vikings were old enough to drink beer," he sneered. "You might get drunk but your mummies and daddies can't help you. They're the other side of the sea!"

Offa, a Saxon with a hard face and mean eyes, pushed forward.

"Why don't you lot build your little boat and go home? Good riddance! We'll be glad to see the back of you!"

His friends closed up. Some clenched small rocks in their fists. But before Vimp could respond, Lief sprang to his feet to calm things.

"Listen!" he implored. "We can be friends. The other Saxon kids accept us. It's just you, Egeslic-and your gang."

A large stone hit the ground centimetres from his foot. Lief recovered his balance and stood firm. But Offa was not finished with him.

"Listen, Viking boy," he snarled. "We never asked you to come here. And we don't want you to stay. You can't even speak our language, properly."

English Emma strode out in front of the two warring groups. She was not taking any more insults, especially from her own people.

"You should be ashamed of yourselves!" she cried. "Vikings are just like us. You know they've never caused you any bother. The ship they're building will be the best for miles. Some of you might even get to sail in it."

The idea did not appeal to Egeslic who hated the sea. He pulled a face and looked disdainfully at the piled timbers.

"You wouldn't catch me going out in it," he jeered. "It'd sink the minute a wind blows up."

He turned his gaze on Emma.

"In any case, why are you mixing with Vikings? You're supposed to be English like us. Everyone knows you're sweet on Poetry Boy."

Egeslic shot a cruel glance in Lief's direction. Emma's blood rushed to her cheeks but Lief held her back.

"Look," he said. "Why don't you move on? You see to your fields and we'll build our boat. Keep out of each other's way. Does that make sense?"

The small group of Saxons closed up. Offa acted as spokesman.

"Fine," he said. "No problem. But you, Lief, or whatever your name is, just keep your hands off Emma. She's English. She shouldn't be messing around with Viking scum."

He stepped forward, raised his right hand and hurled a stone. It struck Lief's cheek. Blood spurted out and a cruel jeer went up from the Saxons. Eric, bold and impulsive, sprang forward and grabbed Offa by the scruff of his neck. His fist sank into the young Saxon's face. The boy fell to the ground, rolling up into a ball before Eric could inflict more damage. Vimp threw himself at Eric and grasped his wrist before he could strike again. Eric's blood was up and Vimp needed help to hold him back. Bristling with anger, the Saxons gathered round Offa to get him to his feet. Blood streamed from his broken nose.

Egeslic fixed Vimp with his steely eyes.

"You've gone too far, Vikings," he growled. "You'll hear more about this. Just wait 'til we get back to Chief Alfred."

He turned to his companions and ordered them away. Offa, sobbing, stumbled back to the village. Vimp released his grip on Eric's arm and pushed him away. He ran over to Lief to find Emma caring for his flesh wound.

"I'm all right," Lief spluttered. "It's my fault. I should have ignored them. Let me take the blame."

Disturbed by the sudden violence, the young Vikings reluctantly returned to their labours but found it hard to work with enthusiasm. As the afternoon wore on, they knew they would have to face the wrath of Alfred. The village Chieftain was known to be a fair man but they could not imagine he would side with them. Far more likely, Alfred would favour the version spun to him by the Saxons. No one looked forward to returning to the huts. It seemed Eric had got himself, and his fellow Vikings, into serious trouble.

* * * *

CHAPTER THREE

Black Dog Of The Forest

Vimp and his shipwright friends worked hard on their boat for the Saxons. First, the keel got laid and, after that, the seasoned timbers filled out the curve of the boat. Freya thought it looked like a dead giant's skeleton. She had once seen the remains of a washed up whale. Over the months, its flesh was picked by crows and wolves. Eventually, the bones of the rib cage stood out along the backbone. Flooded by the tides, the skeleton took months to break up. Now, in England, she watched something grow, rather than rot.

Her mind flashed back to another time when Freya, the longboat her friends named after her, had been set on fire at a Viking funeral. In it lay the dead body of Agnar, Chief of Wolves. With his gallant brothers, Agnar had battled with the legendary Fenris-Wolf to save Freya's life. After her rescue, and with the boat safely back in England, wounded Agnar died. He was given a sea funeral.

"Our boys never stop," she thought. "All that sawing and hammering. Their row drives me crazy."

The vessel was built as a present to the good-hearted Saxon villagers. After the face-up with the village louts, Freya had been smart. She sought out the people's Leader before they could get to him. Alfred listened, knowing the Viking girl always told the truth. He was also aware that Egeslic was a nasty bully and it worried him.

"First, Freya, I must speak to Vimp and his friends," said Alfred. "Even if they feel they were set up, they're still here as our guests. You Vikings must learn to settle."

Later, in his quiet way, the village Leader took Vimp and Eric aside and ordered them to keep out of further trouble.

"It's you I worry about, young Eric," he said. "You work hard and your heart is honest but you have a hot temper. Try not to get into arguments. If it happens again, we shall tell you to leave. You're tall and strong so there's no need to fight. Cool heads settle fights better than fists."

Eric stood awkwardly before the Saxon Leader, shifting his weight from one foot to the other. He knew he had let his friends down.

"I promise I'll control my hot blood," he told Alfred. "And make up with Egeslic."

Late in the afternoon, Eric set out for the forest. He wanted to cool off and find time to think.

"Problem is," he thought, "I seem to get myself into trouble without meaning to. I just don't get it."

What Eric did not realise was that he was always the person who stood up for people. He despised bullies and would not be pushed around. Penetrating deep into the forest, he kept to the worn track. The light began to fade but he had no thoughts of turning back. Little by little, a soft darkness crept through the trees as the sun's rays weakened. Eric came suddenly to his senses.

"It must be time to return," he decided. "The others will be wondering where I am."

Longer shadows fell across the track but Eric was confident he could find his way home. He had been away longer than he appreciated and his stomach told him it was supper time. Up ahead, a young deer sprang through the dense undergrowth. Eric caught only the briefest glance as it crossed the path.

"Total panic," Eric smiled.

He stopped to listen but the forest was silent with no bird singing in the evening light. Why was the deer so desperate to break cover?

A curious sound…over to his right and hard to make out. A low rumbling…nearer now. Some creature pushing its way through dense vegetation? Eric detected the sharp snapping of twigs. Something or someone, certainly. A hunting party? Surely not at this time of day.

Eric Bignose, bravest of Vikings, stood motionless. Behind him…all of a sudden… a deep growl. He broke out in cold sweat. The heavy crashing grew nearer. Eric looked round for escape. Which way to turn?

"Up this tree!"

Grasping a branch, he hauled himself into an ancient oak.

"I'll crawl along the main branch and hide amongst the leaves…"

Snaking his way along the twisted limb of the oak, Eric found cover, and clung on for dear life. He peered through the leaves to see a huge, shaggy bear on the path. It was followed by a smaller creature. Dark, furry… a cub. But the hidden Viking sensed the parent was anxious to be on its way. The cub padded behind.

"Arghhh! Arghhh!"

A blood-chilling snarl; harsh, cruel. The mother bear turned to face the direction of the threat. Her cub hid behind her.

"Arghhh!"

The bear reared up on her hind legs, baring powerful, white teeth. Eric heard her panting. She dropped down on all fours and backed away. Her gaze remained fixed ahead whilst Eric, up in his refuge, squirmed round to find the reason for the bear's distress. What he saw made the small hairs on his neck stand up. He gripped tightly onto the branch, fearing he might fall.

From out of the trees, appeared an extraordinary creature. It was like nothing he had ever seen, dreamed or imagined. Jet black, almost wolf-like. An animal every bit as large as the mother bear. Long hair; gaping mouth. Awesome fangs, dripping with saliva. The bear rumbled a deep warning. Her opponent snarled, viciously.

The monster sat back on its haunches, about to spring at the mother who stood between it and her cub. Raising her head, she prepared for battle. With a blood-curdling growl, the huge black dog flung itself on the exposed neck of the bear. They rolled over and over as each sought to find a weak spot. But as the mighty struggle continued, the bear's strength sapped and its wild attacker got on top. Its deadly jaws clamped onto the bear's neck. Slowly, the mother's life drained away.

Motionless on his high perch, Eric stared down on the saddest of scenes. The mother was mortally wounded. Of the cub, there was no trace. It had fled to the surrounding forest. The black dog released its grip. Its red tongue hung from its mouth as it panted for breath. The beast seemed satisfied with its victory and stood over bear's final twitches. It raised its head and howled into gathering gloom. Turning on its tracks, the creature padded away.

Up in the tree, Eric found his limbs shaking. It took courage to venture down. He avoided the body of the dead bear but kept a sharp look-out for the black beast. Unarmed, Eric knew he was no match.

The trees seemed to close in on all sides. Hurrying silently along the path, Eric became aware of a small movement in the bracken. He froze, unable to control his heart rate. The fronds parted and out onto the path stumbled a small bear. It was lost and bewildered, still seeking its mother. Eric heaved a huge sigh of relief. He noticed the youngster held its ground but was not aggressive. Very gingerly, he approached the cub and knelt down. The little bear lifted its shaggy head and sniffed at him. Eric reached out and the bear shuffled forwards. He touched its ears and laid his hands on its furry neck. He spoke to it, quietly, and the cub appeared to relax.

"I can't leave you here, little one. You'll never survive on your own."

Eric calmed the animal by stroking its back. The bear nuzzled into him.

"Will you let me lift you?"

He knew mother bears sometimes carried their young. Very carefully, he placed his hands under the chest and raised the cub to his shoulder. Its sharp claws gripped onto him.

"Better be going," he said. "Out of this forest. It can't be far."

Eric continued down the track but, with every step, he was aware of something following. Shadowing every step, so it seemed.

"It's imagination," he told himself. "There's nothing there. If I'm going to be attacked it would have happened before now."

But there was something there. In the fading light, Eric made out the shape of a dark object blocking his path. He swallowed hard. The creature did not move but its eyes glowed. At first, yellow, then blood red. Eyes the size of saucers. Eric gripped onto the cub. There was no escape.

As swiftly as it had appeared, the creature turned and disappeared into the darkness. The way was open and Eric ran towards the bright lights of village fires.

"Come on, cub," he whispered hoarsely. "We'll get there together. You've been really brave."

For the first time in his bold life, Eric the Brave had faced terror. A fear far worse than the pirates' attacks, at sea. Or the time Aegir, God of the Oceans, had raised his fist and threatened to crush his boat. He shuddered. A black monster of a dog whose huge eyes glowed horribly in the dark. A creature capable of killing a full-grown bear. Eric was thankful to get back to safety. He entered the village with the cub dangling round his shoulder.

* * * *

CHAPTER FOUR

Forest Mission

"Are you crazy?"

Vimp could hardly hold back.

"You've got us into all sorts of bother with the Saxons. Then you disappeared and no one knew where to look for you. Astrid was so upset. Don't you ever think about anyone except yourself?"

Eric gently levered the bear cub from his shoulders and held it to his chest.

"Listen, Vimp, I'm sorry. I was angry and just had to get out of the village. It drives me mad."

Vimp was not impressed.

"That's the way you see it," he said grumpily. "You're the one person stopping us from settling. You don't see it, do you?"

Eric cast his eyes to the ground.

"I know," he agreed. "I got it wrong again. I'll try to do better."

Eric saw the look of disbelief in Vimp's eyes, fixed on the bear cub. They were joined by the other boys and girls but the cub held centre stage.

"With respect, Eric," Leif said quietly, "the last thing this village needs is a bear from the forest. You can't keep it."

Eric felt foolish.

"I know," he said. "But what was I supposed to do? Its mother's dead and it can't look after itself. I think it's still feeding on milk."

He shuffled his feet.

"I look after the cows and goats. There's always a drop of milk spare. When the cub grows, I'll find it stuff in the forest."

Astrid came to his rescue although she sounded upset.

"I'm furious with you, Eric Bignose," she stormed. "You're a hopeless case. You can't take the cub back to the forest. It'll have to stay here. But just one problem. What happens when it grows up?"

Eric had not had time to think about this. And he had not yet told them about his scary confrontation with the demon dog. Now did not seem to be the right moment.

"Look! What d'you expect? Do I let it starve?"

Astrid put out a hand. The cub did not appear to mind being stroked.

"I'll help you," she offered. "But have you seen the size of a full grown bear? They get enormous. And this one might not stay friendly."

The others agreed. The bear could stay for now. But the sooner it was returned to the forest, the better. And what would the Saxons think? This was one more excuse to set them against the young Vikings.

The group stood in the light of the flickering flames, illuminating the darkness.

"We'll have to make a cage for it," Lief suggested. "But it'll need exercise. How on earth will you stop it getting loose?"

Eric's friends were at a loss for an answer although they were warming to the orphan. Vimp suggested getting hold of a leather collar like the ones the Saxons used for their boar hounds.

"We could ask the blacksmith to knock us up a chain," he said. "I'm sure we'll cope."

By now, the friends were in agreement. Seeing the sleepy cub nestling in Eric's strong arms made them feel happy.

"It could be our mascot," Lief suggested. "We need to think of a name for him…'

"Or her," Ingrid interrupted.

They laughed. Being in charge of a bear cub suddenly seemed like fun but, in their excitement, no one had spotted Eric was still shaking. They had no idea of his recent escape.

"We'd better turn in," Vimp said. "Our boat's nearly complete, but it's up early in the morning. And there are animals to see to. I guess your bear should sleep in our hut, tonight. Only one night, mind you," he added firmly.

The girls crowded round and took turns to touch the little animal on its rough neck.

"It's sweet," said Ingrid. "I'll forgive you!"

Wishing each other good night, they turned and went their separate ways. Lief, always the quick thinker, hurried off to find a spot of goat's milk for the new arrival.

"Beowulf," he thought to himself. "That's the name for the bear."

He pulled back the leather curtain at the hut entrance he shared with Vimp and Eric. The wick of a mutton fat candle gave out a feeble flame.

"Try this."

He offered a small wooden mug of goat's milk to Eric who sat bolt upright with Beowulf in his lap.

"Maybe if you dip your finger in, the cub will suck?" Lief suggested.

He could not help chuckling, quietly, as he watched the tough Viking boy coax the young bear to lick his milky fingers. Lief's mind went back to the time when Eric had carried the wounded body of Agnar, the wolf. Agnar had fought courageously to rescue Freya from the fangs of a monster. Once more, Eric the Bold was revealing his tender side. Lief noticed the cub showed interest in the warm milk. Soon, it fell asleep. Gently, Eric placed it on straw. Lief smiled and blew out the flame.

Next morning, a gathering of Village leaders, young and old, met in the large, communal hut. They sat on rough benches round a fire of crackling logs. Smoke drifted aimlessly up to the hole at the centre of the grimy thatch. Eric and Vimp stood before Chief Alfred. Grim Saxon faces glowered at them.

"We've called you before us because a serious story has leaked out."

The Chief pointed at Eric.

"You!" he said. "The boy who wandered into the forest."

Alfred paused and turned to his companions.

"And returned with a bear cub. We understand its mother is dead. Our interest, however, is not in the cub. We heard you confronted another creature?"

The tall, young Viking ran his hand through his knotted locks. He coughed, wood smoke catching at the back of his throat. It was hard explaining in new Saxon words.

"It's true," he said. "I went alone. On my return, an adult bear and its cub crossed my path. I shinned up the nearest tree. Then…"

Eric's voice trailed off. He swallowed hard.

"It was horrible. Indescribable. A black beast. It went for the adult bear and killed it. Later, when I neared the village, the thing slunk out from the bushes to bar my way."

A cold shiver ran down his spine.

"I thought it was about to attack me but it stayed still. Staring at me with those eyes. It was getting dark. I was really scared."

Anselm, a highly respected elder, spoke up.

"Describe the creature, young man."

Eric hesitated but Chief Alfred insisted he went on.

"Black," Eric stammered. "As big as the bear. Difficult to make out in the dark but… maybe… like a dog. Wolf, even. Terrifying teeth…"

He dried up.

"Go on," Anselm encouraged.

"The beast fixed me with its cold eyes," Eric told him. "Huge. Glowing in the dark. First yellow; then red. I was so scared I can't be sure."

"Anselm is a wise man," Alfred said. "We ask for his explanation."

The elderly Saxon rose awkwardly to his feet, supported by a wooden stick. Stroking his wispy, greying beard, he addressed the assembly.

"What we've heard from this young man disturbs me. I don't blame him. This could have happened to any of us. Evil forces are at work. Forces of the Devil, I suspect."

The hut rang with anxious voices. Chief Alfred called for order and begged Anselm to continue.

"I can't be sure," he said slowly. "But I suggest this appearance may take us back to the times of our ancestors. The days when the first Saxons sailed to these shores and brought their beliefs. Gods of the North and Spirits and Devils. Today, some worship the Christian God. Few bother with the old Gods. But I know one who does. We must find him and ask for guidance."

Anselm looked Alfred squarely in the eye.

"Don't ask me questions, Alfred. You mustn't enquire where this person lives. We seek ancient wisdom and I can't give you his name. Above all, the Christian Priest who visits should not be told of this. He'd say we are pagans; not believing in his Christian God but in the spirits of the woods. The beliefs of our ancestors. I shall need escorts."

The old man wobbled on his stick and had to be helped to his bench. Chief Alfred thanked him.

"This conversation must not go beyond these walls. No villager should hear of it. It would create panic. We're dealing with dangerous forces few of us understand. I grant Anselm permission to seek the person he speaks of."

Alfred looked round the small gathering.

"I ask for need volunteers," he said. "Four freemen to accompany Anselm on a dangerous mission."

No one spoke up. Men looked down at their earthen floor hoping not to be noticed. Vimp stepped forward.

"I'll go," he said.

"And me," said Eric, unhesitating.

Two Saxon brothers leapt to their feet.

"Count us in," one cried. "Two Saxons and two Vikings. That's a match for anyone, human or spirit. We'll look after Anselm. My name is Leofwine!"

Even Eric was impressed at the size of the broad-chested young man, straggles of long hair over his craggy face.

"And this is my brother, Eadbehrt."

A younger man strode forward. His beard and moustache hid his mouth but the young Vikings detected a gleam in his eyes.

"Nothing frightens me," he claimed, fingering the dagger at his belt. "I chased wolves off my sheep, last week. They haven't been back since. One black dog means nothing. I'll take on a whole pack!"

The Meeting broke up leaving Chief Alfred and Anselm with their new comrades. Alfred was grateful to the brave Saxons.

"Don't take your task lightly," he warned. "Listen well to Anselm and take his instructions."

Early next morning at the crowing of the cockerels, the forest party met in the first light. Despite his need for a walking stick, Anselm seemed as ready as his younger companions. Each traveller carried bread and salted meat, bundled in a cloth. Vimp and Eric had hardly slept. It had not been possible to tell their friends they were leaving. Or the reason why. The young Vikings marvelled at how relaxed the Saxon brothers appeared. Leofwine and Eadbehrt were taken by Eric's bear cub. Anselm regarded it more gravely.

"It seems to have adopted you," he said. "I see you have a flagon of milk, at your waist."

He looked thoughtfully at the small animal.

"Bears are special creatures. No braver beast inhabits the forest. This small animal may prove helpful on our journey."

The adventurers lifted the wooden bar securing the main gate and headed across the nearest pasture. Hopping ahead of them, in the emerging light, a scruffy black crow scavenged its first meal of the day. Crows were bad news. Saxon and Viking, they had all listened to stories passed down by their forebears. The big bird pierced them with a sharp look from its beady eye and flapped away, over the trees.

"That's an unfortunate start," thought Vimp. "Was it sent to spy on us?"

The party entered the wood, in single file. Unusually for the time of the year, the forest was silent. Eadbehrt, guided by Anselm, led the way with the two Viking boys following. Thoughtful Leofwine posted himself at the rear. They plunged deeper into the forest, occasionally resting at a stream to drink. These moments gave Anselm time to plan the next step.

"I've made this journey only once before," he told his companions. "But I'm fairly sure of my way, and sense we're being guided. You can be certain we're also being watched by the Spirits of the Old Gods. This is their world and we human folk are not especially welcome. Treat them with respect."

Big Eric was beginning to feel more himself. The shock of the previous day had faded and he felt confident to take on the world. Beowulf the Bear trailed behind, never allowing his new parent out of sight. Secretly, Eric was pleased to see it strayed off the path to snuffle amongst old tree roots. It was learning to feed itself.

"There is something you must know," said Anselm as his escorts enjoyed thirst-quenching apples. "I'm not who you think I am."

He paused. A hush descended over the forest glade through which bubbled a winding stream.

"Tomorrow, a new priest comes to our village. He's found out about my past and isn't likely to be my friend. He may order that I leave."

The younger Saxons and Vikings craned forward. Not one took a bite from his apple.

"I was once respected more than I am, today. Now, only Alfred seems to treat me properly. You see…"

He paused and looked round his friends.

"There was a time when sick people sought me out. Took my advice and drank my medicines."

The old man closed his eyes, remembering his younger days.

"I was close to the spirits of the forest. You see the tall Ash tree over there; its branches stretching ever upwards?"

Anselm rose slowly his feet and walked over. Stretching out his hands, he felt the rough bark and bent down to pick up a twig.

"This tree is special," he called back. "It connects our world with the times of ancient Gods. The Gods shared by Old Saxon folk and Viking peoples. We worshipped them before the Christian God was forced upon us."

He held the slender branch before him described a circle through the air.

"With this wand I can fend off bad spirits," he said. "Whatever happens, or whatever you see during the next few hours, you must always keep secret."

Anselm's companions stayed silent, not daring to challenge the elderly man. They watched, in awe, as he touched the branch on the ground. No one moved a muscle as he drew a circle in the dusty earth. He stood in the centre.

"We're now protected from serpents," he said. "The bite of the adder can no longer harm you."

He raised the branch in front of his wrinkled face. The escorts stood, transfixed, as Anselm sang a tuneless chant in his old, cracked voice.

"I stand in this circle to guard against the venom of the serpent. We worshippers shall permit no evil to enter our souls. We fear nothing and seek and trust the trees who are our friends.

And the timeless rocks, blessed with goodness. Likewise, the springs of pure water."

Even Eric kept his silence. Anselm stepped gingerly out of his sacred circle and re-joined his companions. The Ash branch remained in his hand.

"Do not be afraid," he said. "Tell no human what you have seen. Our ancestors respected these trees and creatures."

The travellers gathered their bits and pieces then plunged deeper into the mysteries of the enchanted forest.

* * * *

CHAPTER FIVE

The Stagman

The woodland explorers reached parts of the forest where only the boldest hunters dare venture. It was necessary to slash at brambles arching across the ancient path. Eric's hands and arms soon became scarred by the sharp thorns, drawing blood. He began to wonder if the old man knew where he was going.

Beowulf tagged along. He seemed happy with his new parent, never letting him out of his sight. But, all of a sudden, the cub stopped and whimpered. His master turned and knelt down at his side.

"What's up, little one? Are you getting tired? I could carry you but I think your mother would've made you carry on."

The bear uttered a feeble growl. Eric could not help laughing.

"I'm getting complaints," he informed the group. "An angry bear. I don't know if I can handle this!"

Anselm turned and looked at the cub with interest.

"Hush!" he advised. "Respect your wild friend. Remember… he knows far more about these woods than we can ever know. He's trying to tell us something."

Vimp glanced at Eric who suddenly looked anxious.

"Up ahead," he whispered. "Did something move?"

Anselm held the Ash branch in front of his chest. Then he whisked it back and forth.

"Clever cub," he said quietly. "Pick him up. He needs comforting."

Big Eric bent down and placed his strong hands under the bear's belly. He felt Beowulf tremble.

Anselm called loudly to the trees.

"Begone, evil presence!"

He wafted his branch and the two Saxons joined him. They were anxious to know what was going on.

"Fear not," Anselm replied. "This Ash protects us. But keep your eyes open. The journey was never going to be easy."

Leofwine remembered the wise words of Chief Alfred. Anselm had to be obeyed.

"We move on!"

Anselm was determined to continue his mission. For the next two hours, the small band plunged further into the forest. Vimp felt uneasy. It was as though something, or someone, was following them just out of sight. There was never anything to see. Just a hint. An occasional shaking of leaves.

"I'm being stupid," he told himself.

Looking at Eric did not put him at his ease. He knew his fearless friend was tense. Eric clutched Beowulf to his chest. There was no way the cub could be put down again. Up ahead, Anselm raised his hand and signalled a stop.

"We're close," he said. "All is well. Look out, now, for a large grey rock. Or you may first hear the stream. It bubbles from a well in a sacred place. Only here can we be close to the spirits."

Anselm's words failed to comfort Eric and Vimp. They agreed they should have remained in the village. It seemed so far away. Another world.

It was Eadbehrt who spotted the first signs. Hacking his way through vegetation growing over the track, he stopped and pointed to a small Birch tree.

"What's that hanging on its branches?" he asked. "Like... little pieces of cloth. Pale blues; reds. Looks as though they've been there for ages."

He shook his head in bewilderment.

"Who'd want to do that?" he went on.

Eadbehrt was right. Tatty pieces of torn cloth fluttered from the lower branches of the tree. He saw they had been tied on but were now bleached by the sun and rain.

"Listen!"

The others fell quiet. From not far away they heard the liquid gurgling of water rising from the earth. And, as they approached, they came upon a huge boulder covered in moss. Tall ferns sprang from its crevices.

"We've arrived," Anselm announced. "Our journey's been rewarded. Treat this spot with respect. We're with the spirits of the forest. They'll not harm us."

Vimp remained unconvinced. He had little time for the old Viking Gods. So it was even harder to get worked up about Anglo-Saxon 'spirits' belonging to a bygone age. He circled the rock, cautiously, and discovered crystal clear water springing from its heart. Anselm signalled his comrades to sit.

"Rest awhile," he said. "Refresh yourselves. Wash your faces and tired limbs. Your energies will be restored. For my part, I must leave you. Have no fear. I shan't be long."

He looked at each young adventurer, in turn.

"When I come back, you must be brave. Hold your ground and don't be tempted to flee. If you do, you'll get lost in the trees. Only I can find the way back."

His wizened old face broke into a twisted smile.

"Trust me," he insisted, "All will be well."

Anselm turned and hobbled past the mysterious rock. His nervous companions looked on as he prodded the uneven ground with his walking stick. Leofwine went over to the stream and sniffed the air.

"This is a weird place," he said thoughtfully. "Our lives are in Anselm's hands."

Late in the afternoon, Anselm reappeared through the trees, stick in one hand and wand in the other. He walked slowly as Vimp jumped to his feet to greet him.

"You had us worried," he said. "We were beginning to wonder...'

The old man raised one hand and waved the walking stick.

"I told you to have faith," he said. "There's much to tell you. Pack up your things."

The final part of the journey did not take long. The air grew cooler. Gaunt trees pressed in from all sides. Eric clutched Beowulf even tighter. A snake with zig-zig markings on its back slithered from the path. It made no attempt to bite.

"Stop!"

Anselm raised his arm..

"Go carefully," he advised. "You're now in the presence of the spirits. They see your every move. Behave with respect and say nothing."

He shuffled on. In front, was a small clearing of wild grasses where sunlight penetrated the woodland. To one side, Vimp spotted a cave hollowed from the cliff above. Anselm lowered himself on his knees and signalled for the others to do the same. The younger travellers laid their packs on the ground and knelt in an untidy line. At first, Eric did not notice the breeze that caused the leaves to rustle. He felt a cold draught on his cheek. Leofwine's unruly black hair blew across his face. He swept it back but the breeze increased.

Bushes and smaller trees at the edge of the clearing began to sway. The whole forest seemed alive as the gathering wind swept fallen leaves into a swirl, dashing them against the kneelers' faces. Vimp flung his arms up to protect his eyes. The wind ceased almost as soon as it had begun. When he reopened his eyes he did not believe what he saw. From the mouth of the cave emerged a figure, taller than a man. Although it walked upright and on two legs, it appeared more animal than human. Stag's antlers protruded from its head. The face, too, was that of a deer but looked unreal, like a mask. The figure wore deerskin tied by leather thongs. It raised two arms and lifted its animal head to the sun. Vimp and Eric knelt, icy shivers running down their spines. Never in their adventurous lives had they been so terror-struck. The bear cub gave a pitiful cry and buried deep into his master's chest. Even Anselm did not dare look up. Head bowed, he cast his eyes humbly to the ground.

The half-human, half-animal creature stepped towards the petrified visitors. It spoke in a deep, throaty rumble.

"You dare enter this sacred place? You are not invited. Nor are you welcome, except Anselm. Because he has brought you here I, Wizard of the Forest, will aid you. I do not sense you hold to our ancient beliefs. You may believe in the new God. I do not know Him. My wisdom is gained from your ancestors."

Vimp stood rooted to the spot.

"Anselm has told me of your plight. One of you has been tempted by great evil. This may bring disaster upon him, his friends and family. None can escape."

Eric raised his head, fractionally. The Stagman's blazing eyes glared at him.

"I'm that one," he whispered hoarsely. "Blame me and not the rest. I'm ready to take my punishment."

The Stagman approached Eric and touched him on the shoulder.

"You are brave," he said. "You are from the Norse lands."

The Wizard reached into a large bag dangling from a belt, around his middle. One by one, he pulled out small objects and laid them in the dust. First, a buzzard's flight feather. Then three rounded pebbles which he laid in the shape of a triangle.

"This feather was given to me by a fine bird of these woods," he said. "I place it inside the stones. Its magic fights demons who may attempt to possess your souls."

Then the Wizard took out several small bones. He held each one before Eric's face, returning them to the pouch. Eric shuddered as the Wizard placed his deerskin-covered hands on his shoulders.

"Come with me!" he commanded. "I ask Anselm to be my witness."

Eric rose to his feet and handed Beowulf to Vimp.

"Bring the bear cub with you," the Wizard told him. "He is your best protection."

The Stagman sensed Eric's reluctance but insisted on obedience.

"The animal will not be harmed," he said. "The day may come when it will return the kindness you showed it."

The Stagman turned and walked slowly towards his cave. Eric and Anselm followed. He invited them into the gloomy interior where a small fire smouldered in one corner. Over the fire stood a tripod from which hung a blackened iron cauldron. The cave smelt of smoke and woodland scents.

"Take this cup!"

The Stagman handed Eric a wooden vessel then stood by the boiling pot, turning his hands to the rising steam.

"Heal and mend this broken spirit," he intoned. "Drive away all poisons that have entered his poor soul."

He bent to pick up a small bunch flowers, picked from the glade.

"This is Mugwort," he said, gravely.

Holding the slender fronds of the wayside plant in the fire smoke, the Stagman broke off its tiny flowers and tossed them into the pot. He picked up a large spoon.

"With this sacred instrument I stir my potion. Once cooled, you must drink."

The big Viking boy gulped.

"I can't!" he protested. "It smells horrible. You can't force me!"

Anselm raised his old eyebrows.

"Obey," he advised. "No harm will befall you."

The Stagman spooned out steaming, green liquid into a cup. After a short while, he raised it to Eric's lips.

"Drink!" he commanded. "Waste not a drop. I travelled to the Other World to learn the secrets of this potion!"

Eric submitted to swallow the most awful drink he had ever tried. The hot liquid scorched his mouth and throat. He felt sick but fought to hold down the sacred, herbal mixture. Anselm placed a comforting arm on his shoulder.

"You acted bravely, my son. Now, we can return in peace and hope."

Eric staggered out of the cave, clutching his stomach. His bear trotted, behind.

"Beowulf the Bear!" the Stagman called from his cave entrance. "I know your name. It means 'The Bee Wolf. He who attacks bees. Guard your friend with your life."

Eric struggled back to his friends, clutching at his stomach. Anselm spoke to calm them.

"What you have seen today, you have not seen. Neither have you heard what you have heard. Tell no-one of these events."

He bowed gravely towards the cave, before turning towards the path.

"Follow me," he commanded. "And forget!"

The comrades did as they were told. Vimp glanced back but the cave had vanished. Like its strange inhabitant, it was no longer to be seen.

* * * *

CHAPTER SIX

Black Shuck

"You people are pagan fools! You continue to worship spirits that never existed. There is only One God. Only He may be worshipped. No other."

The wooden church in the Saxon village rang with the strong words of Wilfred, the newly-appointed Priest. Sent from the nearby Abbey, he thundered at the gathering of humble folks before him.

"None of you are worthy of God's love. Yet Our Lord is forgiving."

The young man in the brown robe stood before the altar. Turning his shaven head to Heaven, he asked God's blessing on the people who knelt with bowed heads.

"Show mercy to these simple sheep who have lost their way."

Wilfrid looked grimly at his new flock.

"Little did I realise," he said, "that when I came to your village, I would be amongst wicked heathen."

A feeling of dread passed through the packed congregation. It was the first time Eric had attended the church he and his Viking friends had helped build. Now, they knelt with the Saxons.

The Priest fingered the white rope tied around his middle.

"Do you seriously believe trees and animals can be worshipped? That a rock is sacred and your forest full of demons? I understand that a young man, amongst you, claims to have confronted a creature of great evil. What rubbish! He's making it up."

Wilfrid faced his humbled audience.

"I hear he's a Viking. You've shown him and his friends great kindness. See how he repays you."

Eric began to feel uneasy. The Priest was turning the whole village against him. A wild feeling of panic welled up. He rose to his feet and pointed angrily at the Priest.

"What do you know? You weren't there. I know what I saw. That black dog was a demon. It killed a bear!"

The Saxons shook their heads, in dismay. The young Viking was insulting their new Priest. Brother Wilfrid stood in front of Eric.

"How dare you speak like this in God's house? We've been told you and some others entered a forbidden part of the forest. You consulted a Wizard who hides in a cave."

A murmur of outrage swept through the gathering.

"And," the Priest stormed on, "a senior member of our community led you there!"

All eyes turned on the kneeling Anselm who kept his eyes down.

"You are young. This man misled you. Anselm consulted with spirits that don't exist. That world that has passed. Only the Christian God can conquer evil. It was to Him you should have turned."

"I'm not a Christian so I wouldn't know!" Eric announced brazenly.

His outburst shocked the worshippers.

"Brother Wilfrid is right!" one called out. "He's a heathen. We should be rid of him. He's a curse upon us. Ban Vikings from our village!"

Old Anselm struggled to his feet. He raised his stick to the noisy congregation.

"These young people are not to blame," he shouted over the noise. "It's true I led them to the forest. But I did it for a reason. Eric tells the truth. The Demon Dog of legend is amongst us. It stalks our village, at night. What does the Christian God know of this? Only by consulting the ancient spirits can this Demon be got rid of."

A farmer leapt to his feet and struck Anselm on the head. The blow toppled the old man whose stick crashed to the floor. Anselm fell and lay lifeless. Vimp and Bjorne hurried to him but did not need telling he was dead.

"God have mercy on us all!"

The Priest raised his voice to the wooden rafters of the roof as the people recoiled from the scene. The farmer stood transfixed, horrified at his violent action. His friends shrank away and women wept. Astrid and Ingrid hurried to Eric.

"Come away," Astrid, clamping his arms. "It's not safe...'

She did not finish her sentence. A piercing scream went up from the back of the church. The door burst open and a wind howled through the building. A hideous wolf-like creature stood at the doorway. Parents clutched their children. The beast exposed its yellow fangs; evil eyes glowing with menace. In a single bound, it leapt at the throat of the Priest. Then turned and glared at the worshippers crowding behind the altar.

The monster sprang at the open church door, its awful claws scorching marks into the ancient oak. The villagers fell on their knees, crossing themselves and seeking God's protection. The Demon Dog turned and fled the building.

A small group gathered round the frail body of Anselm whilst others ran over to the Priest. But it was hopeless. The young man lay where he died without a mark on his throat. An Elder, shaking as he spoke, called for silence.

"Anselm was right," he said. "Our community is haunted. We have seen The Black Shuck!"

All knew the legend of The Shuck from childhood. Terrifying tales of the beast had been passed down the generations. Only magic could rid the village of its threat.

* * * *

CHAPTER SEVEN

Eric's Departure

Frightened families left the church, clinging for comfort. The Saxons were horrified at the slaughter of the new Priest. Some felt guilt, expecting their new God to send down punishment. They hurried home, avoiding the young Vikings. Meanwhile, Vimp and company trudged back to their shelters. Astrid held onto Eric, offering support, but knew he felt responsible for the dramatic events. Beowulf got up to greet his new friends and Astrid fondled his ears.

Eric collapsed onto his mattress. Nothing made sense. How could he be at fault for what had happened? The situation was out of control. Vimp offered a drink but he refused.

"I can't stay here," he said unhappily. "I bring bad luck. Far better for me to leave so you can all settle with the Saxons."

Vimp did not agree.

"If you go, we all go," he replied. "It isn't fair you should take the blame."

Lief agreed. Astrid felt desperate for the boy she admired.

"Somehow," Lief said, "we've to get the Saxons back on side. There must be something we can do."

No-one came up with any suggestions. They sat, silently, in the semi-darkness with their own thoughts. It was not long before a small party of Saxon leaders stood at the curtained entrance.

"Eric Bignose," one called out loudly, "you're summoned before the Village Court. You're to come, alone."

The tall, young Viking rose to his feet.

"Look after Beowulf," he said. "I must face my fate."

He pulled back the curtain, blinking in the bright afternoon light. Leofwine and Eadbehrt were amongst the group. He shot Astrid a parting glance. In the Community Hut, he was dismayed to see Chief Alfred and the Elders assembled. Alfred wasted no time although he treated Eric with respect.

"We're sorry to have to call for you," he said, gravely. "You've done much since your arrival. But you must realise you now place us in a difficult situation."

Eric stood upright, holding his head high.

"Leofwine and Eadbehrt have spoken up for you," Alfred went on. "They told us of the journey into the forest. Perhaps poor Anselm was mistaken. We understand he sought a certain person in contact with the forest spirits?"

Eric nodded, humbly.

"I have to say," said Alfred, "Anselm did us no favours. But I blame myself for this as I was the one who let him go. Whatever took place in the forbidden part didn't work. The evil wasn't got rid of and now haunts the village."

Leofwine stepped forward.

"With your permission, Alfred," he said, "my brother and I are equally guilty. We all ended up at the cave and saw what went on."

The Chieftain looked round at the small group of Elders.

"It was not you, Leofwine," he said, "who first encountered The Black Shuck. We also understand Eric drank a magic potion prepared by the Wizard. That was foolish and it certainly did no good. The Demon Dog attacked our village. A holy Priest lies dead."

It was true. The Saxon brothers could not argue. Alfred drew himself up to his full height.

"Unless there's anyone here to challenge me, I order Eric Bignose to leave our village at dawn. We'll help him with a parcel of food and he may take anything that belongs to him. On no account, should he approach our community again. He is banned for life!"

A dull murmur of agreement sounded from the Elders. Leofwine and Eadbehrt looked on, sadly, knowing there was nothing they could do. Eric's troubled mind was spinning. He hardly grasped the Chief's stern words.

"You must go," Alfred said. "May God protect you."

The Saxon brothers took Eric gently by the arm and led him back to the hut. Invited inside, they explained what they had heard.

"We promise," they said, "to see Eric through the dangerous part of the forest."

Turning to the shocked Vikings - Vimp, Astrid and Lief - they smiled sadly and left.

No-one slept that night. Eric tossed and turned on his straw, fearing what might befall him. No friends; no Astrid. Only his bear. He stretched out and fondled the cub.

"At least you and I'll stay together, Beowulf," he whispered.

For Vimp and the other boys the situation was unreal. Their hero, Eric the Brave, was being sent away. They could not fathom the reason. He was innocent and it was hardly his fault the Black Shuck had chanced upon him. In her own hut, Ingrid held a sobbing Astrid in her arms. Neither could sleep. Astrid dreaded the dawn; the last day she would see her brave warrior.

A cockerel crowed and a second took up its call as the Saxon village began to wake. Barely able to speak, Vimp and Lief helped Eric put together a shoulder pack. It contained food to get him started and spare clothes.

"I've collected your carpentry kit," said Lief. "Your hand axe, a scraper, chisel, two hammers and the saw. You'll need them to build a shelter. We know you'll survive."

He sounded more confident than he felt. Vimp had been thinking, too.

"Your best bet is to head for the coast," he advised. "I know you. At heart, you're a big softy. I don't see you hunting hares, or deer. And wild forest boars are dangerous customers. You're from a fishing family so you won't need any lessons."

Miserably, they stepped into the grey stillness of the morning. Leofwine and Eadbehrt were waiting for them.

"We don't break promises," they said. "We'll set Eric on his way."

The small group, Beowulf padding along behind, reached the village gate and gazed into the meadow. A thin mist rose from the damp ground, blotting out the distant trees.

"Eric!"

Astrid's cry reached their ears. She ran towards them, holding out a small bundle.

"Apples," she cried. "They're all I could find."

It was clear from her tear-stained face she had wept long into the night. Ingrid came running up, behind her, followed by Freya and Emma.

"We can't believe you're being sent from us!"

The girls hugged the boy as he prepared to leave. Lifting the gate bar, Eric bent and kissed Astrid on her soft cheek.

"I'll never forget you," he told her. "You're my world."

Eric turned to follow the Saxon brothers and did not look back. Tearful Astrid watched as the party disappeared into the mist.

"He's gone!" she said. "I'll never see him again."

The sad youngsters trudged back to the huts. But Vimp's mind was buzzing; partly in anger and partly in despair.

"Let me tell you, Astrid," he said firmly. "If you think I'm letting our Eric go, this easily, you're wrong. I make a vow to find him. Even if I have to track him to the ends of the earth!"

Lief agreed.

"Count me in. Vikings don't let our friends down."

He slipped a comforting arm round Astrid and escorted her back.

"Look after her," he told the other girls. "There's serious thinking to do."

The rising sun dispelled the wet wreaths of mist as the village woke. Cows and sheep were herded out to the meadows whilst women and children fed the geese. The tempting scents of breakfast spread from the roof holes. For the Viking boys, it was yet another busy day, building their sea-going boat. It would not take long to finish and soon be handed over to the Saxons. Freya took Astrid to the family where she helped to care for the children. She kept a close eye on her friend knowing how distressed she was.

Meanwhile, deep into the trees, a gloomy Eric and his Saxon guides headed North. They spoke little, stopping now and again at streams, for a break. Leofwine had been thinking.

"Vimp's right," he said. "No-one can live in this forest by himself. Especially at night. You need to get to the coast."

His brother agreed.

"Remember, Eric, your English speaking gets better, day by day. You're bound to meet people who'll take you in. You're a great sailor and the best boat-builder, ever. We know you have a future!"

The Saxons were right to try to boost Eric's confidence but could not guess at the state of his broken heart.

"I'll get by," he agreed. "But I can't get Astrid out of my mind."

The brothers stayed with the outcast for the rest of the morning. As the trees thinned out, more light penetrated the forest floor. The earth was sandy and the travellers scuffed up clouds of dust. Leofwine stopped to sniff the air.

"I smell the sea," he said. "We're near sand dunes."

Within minutes, they looked over the very bay where the crew of Viking escapers had first landed. Seeing it again brought memories flooding back. Eric remembered how they had heaved the longboat onto the beach. It was in these dunes where an armed bunch of Saxon villagers lay hidden, ready to do battle. Yet these had been the same folks who agreed to let the invaders settle. Now, it seemed that his whole world was turned upside down.

Brave Eric Bignose flexed his aching shoulders and fondled Beowulf's fuzzy head. He turned to his companions.

"I'm on my own, now," he said. "I'm really grateful. You tried your best for me."

He held out his hand and, in turn, shook theirs.

"Don't waste any more time on me. Return to the village."

It was a sad parting. Leofwine looked the brave Viking squarely in the face.

"If you run into trouble with people along here," he said, "remember to mention my name. Leofwine, brother of Eadbehrt; son of Cuichelm."

His brother agreed.

"And mine. Eadbehrt, son of Cuichelm, brother of Leofwine. Our names will keep you safe!"

Thanking them, Eric called to the bear cub who toyed with a piece of driftwood.

"We may meet again," he said. "Look after my friends."

He sighed and stepped boldly into the shingle. The Saxon brothers turned and made their way back to the tree line. There, they looked back but Eric and Beowulf had already disappeared. They slowly plied their way to the village. Few words passed between them.

* * * *

CHAPTER EIGHT

Beowulf's Big Moment

Hardly knowing where he was going, Eric Bignose headed along the coastal path. He looked a sad and forlorn figure, long hair blowing in the stiff breeze. Over his shoulder, he carried his stick and bundle with another bag in his hand. Beowulf held back progress, hurrying off the track to investigate anything new. Every log washed up on the beach had to be turned over; clumps of smelly seaweed turned inside out, disturbing clouds of flies. For the hundredth time, his master called for him to come but Beowulf was not a dog, seeking to please. He had a bear mind of his own. In the end, Eric gave up and saw the funny side.

"We'll never get anywhere at this speed," he scolded the cub.

He realised they were not heading anywhere. The light over the sea began to lose its brightness and Eric knew he had to hole up for his first night. His thoughts flickered back to the village where his friends would be preparing supper. He imagined them sitting huddled round a crackling fire. How was the longboat progressing? To sail it was his great hope, standing at the helm in a strong, following wind. Ocean waves rolling the boat from side to side but the craft always holding steady. It had been put together with all the Viking skill he and his friends could muster.

"It's weird talking to myself," he said out loud. "And chatting to a bear."

Eric reckoned the night would be dry with only a gentle breeze lifting from the sea.

"I'll sleep under the stars and discover what tomorrow brings."

Unpacking his things, he tore a lump out of a hard loaf.

"Here, Beowulf, try this. I've got a piece of pork wrapped up somewhere. We'll need to find a stream. Maybe there's one amongst the trees."

The cub was happy with his supper. When they had finished, boy and bear set out to hunt for water. It did not take long. A small river flowed from the wood and Eric decided to track it.

"It'll be salty as the tide's bound to run up it. If I get up far enough the water may be fresh."

This took longer than he imagined and it was not easy pushing his way through the undergrowth. Suddenly, he noticed the cub was not with him.

"Beowulf!"

He called several times. In the failing light, Eric thrashed around, desperate that the small animal had lost its way. A quick movement in bushes, at the side, caught his eye. Beowulf burst out pursued by angry bees. They swarmed on all sides, burrowing into his thick fur. In his mouth, he carried the remains of a dripping honeycomb. No matter how hard the bees tried to sting, Beowulf held onto his new trophy. He pawed at the boldest attackers. In no time, he devoured what remained of the bees' Winter stores. Eric hid behind a tree and waited for the storm to die down. Backing under a mossy rock, Beowulf managed to survive until the bees lost interest and flew back to the remains of their nest. When he emerged, there was a sticky grin on his face. The bear was extremely pleased with himself.

"You didn't leave any for me," Eric complained. "I could have done with a spot of wild honey!"

Secretly, he was delighted. Beowulf had shown he was able to look after himself, bees or no bees. Eric had no need to worry about feeding him and the clever bear knew when to return. Bending over a stream, the Viking boy cupped his hands and sipped gratefully. The cool water restored his spirits.

Night closed in and he made his way down to the shore. There, he took out his flints and struck a flame, lighting a pile of dry sticks. Adding larger branches from the forest, he soon made a warming fire. There was plenty of driftwood around. Sitting under the starry night sky, Eric felt bolder to face next day's challenges. His bear cub was not so keen on the dancing flames. But he grew brave and nestled close to his master.

"Good night, little one."

Eric stretched out on the thin covering of grass but could not prevent his mind tracking back to his friends. He wondered about Astrid and if she missed him.

The next day, with a freshening wind, Eric and Beowulf set out early. As they walked, the lone Viking planned ahead.

"I've must find a place to settle," he thought. "I can't just go on tramping up this coast. Building a shelter's number one. That's easy as I've got tools. It'll have to be on the edge of a wood. But I don't fancy going into the forest. Then I must set up my fishing. There's plenty of bait in the mud."

He was thinking of the fat sea worms his father used to dig up.

"I've got fish hooks and lines so that shouldn't be a problem. And maybe I could knock up a raft and try river fishing."

A blinding thought flashed into his mind.

"River!" he cried out loud. "That's what I need. A tidal estuary where the sea moves in and out. Just right for fishing."

Packing his bits and pieces, Eric called Beowulf over. To his surprise, the cub obeyed. The outcasts were working as a team.

Eric reached the target he had in mind. Early in the afternoon, he came up against a broad river estuary where water from the land met the sea. As the tide moved out, a huge area of mud flats was left exposed. Divided by winding channels, it smelt salty and rotten and Eric was careful not to get too close. The mud lay thick and treacherous. One slip and he would be in to his waist with no hope of rescue. It was harder keeping Beowulf off the tidal flats. He enjoyed getting covered in mud and came back with a prize; a wriggling eel clamped between his jaws. After a couple of chews the eel disappeared. Beowulf had discovered fish!

Eric gazed out over the dark expanse of liquid mud where small armies of wading birds fed by the water edge. A pair of black and white oyster catchers scudded low over the waves. Eric turned and walked towards the trees.

"This is where I put up our first shelter," he told himself.

By nightfall, the skilled carpenter had selected branches and cut them to size. He bound them with twinings found in the wood. The tall branches met at the top to be tied. His rough, round home would do for the night but more work would be needed. The shelter could never keep out wind or rain. Eric was fortunate. The night stayed dry with only a light breeze blowing off the land. With his food stock dwindling, he knew he would soon have to start fishing.

"I can put a raft together and shape a paddle. Or maybe use a long pole and push up and down on the tide."

He made a fire outside his primitive shack and enjoyed its cheering glow as darkness closed in. Beowulf managed to catch a second eel but also explored the wood for tasty roots and fallen fruits. His master was delighted at the young bear's independence. Dowsing the flames, just in case the wind got up during the night, Eric lay on the soft turf. The bear preferred to sleep outside, disturbing his master with snorts and snuffles.

Was the bear keeping guard? Eric was not sure but it was good to know he had a watchdog.

That night, Eric dreamt of sea journeys. Great battles with mountainous waves and fighting to control the helm. Soaked in salt spray; his brave crew dug their oars into the angry sea. The longboat pitched up and down. An exhausted Astrid huddled against the side. Yet she gazed up at Eric, almost invisible in the storm. She knew he was there and it gave her strength.

The Viking vagabond awoke with a start. Dawn had not yet broken yet he knew where he lay, alone and far from his friends. Big Eric was close to tears. Lying in a make-shift shelter made him depressed. How could he fend for himself with no-one to help? It was at this very moment Beowulf chose to visit his master. The cub ambled into the shelter and pushed his black snout into Eric's face. It smelt curiously of fish and honey. Eric stretched out an arm and fondled the bear's forehead.

"You're a case, bear," the Viking boy told him. "What would I do without you?"

He drifted off to sleep, again, to be woken by the sharp calls of feeding birds on the estuary. The air smelt salty and fresh.

"Lots to do," he thought. "Find some sturdy young trees to build a raft. Bind them together then catch my first fish supper."

Beowulf, too, had been busy. It seemed he had found food and joined Eric by the fire.

"Not afraid of flames, any longer?"

The cub settled by Eric's side as the sun rose over the sea. The rest of the morning was spent at the edge of the wood, selecting raft timbers. He worked hard on a tall ash pole that would propel the craft forward. Back at the hut, he lashed the timbers together and the skilful boat-builder soon made a workable raft. He gathered his fishing lines and hooks.

Unfortunately, he could not persuade Beowulf to join him on board. As Eric pushed off, the cub hurried along the bankside, worried his master might desert him. With the tide running out, Eric tethered his raft in a clump of reeds and let out his lines. He kept a sharp look-out for the bear but need not have worried. Beowulf was busy turning over clumps of seaweed and catching crabs scuttling for cover. Not only did they taste good but they amused him. Meanwhile, his master achieved success when a couple of flatfish took his bait.

"I can't pole back against this tide," Eric thought. "It's too strong so I'll secure the raft and come back for it when the sea's running back in."

Pleased with his haul, he headed for the rickety shelter where he was joined by a happy bear.

"I know this is like an adventure for you, Beowulf," Eric said. "But it's not quite the same for me. I'll just do my best."

Minutes later, he kindled a fire and fixed up a spit of branches from which he could dangle the fish. They were delicious, smoked; the best meal he had ever tasted. Handing scraps to Beowulf, Eric chuckled at the young bear's enthusiasm. It seemed the two had formed a growing bond. Revived by his outdoor lunch, Eric's spirits rose. He went down to the bank of the estuary where he scooped up huge handfuls of runny mud. Most of it ran through his fingers as he hurried back to the shelter.

"I'll daub this disgusting stuff into the gaps between the poles," he thought. "When it hardens it may keep out the rain."

What he had not banked on was how long the work would take. He must have trudged back to the mud flats a hundred times before the shelter even began to look weather-proof.

"I'm exhausted," he thought. "I can't do anymore."

Eric crashed out on the turf of marsh grass as the sun sank over the trees. Nothing could wake him, not even the cub's whimpers.

Beowulf turned his nose into the breeze and sniffed. He smelled danger and padded up and down. Alarmed by sounds beyond the trees, he pushed his black muzzle into his master's face. The drowsy boy came to life.

"What is it?" Eric asked. "What's up?"

He soon found out. Two bearded strangers stepped out from the cover of the trees. They gripped long bows and each carried a quiver of arrows over his shoulder. They were dressed in dull, dirt-stained tunics and leggings. Sharp daggers projected from sheaths at their belts.

Eric rose slowly. He lifted his hands to make clear he had no weapons. The rougher of the men approached.

"Cover me," he ordered the other who slipped an arrow into his bow. He stared suspiciously at the stranger.

"Who are you?" he said. "We don't take to newcomers in these parts."

His companion moved out of the tree cover and trained his bow on the visitor. Eric had been taken by surprise. The first man dropped his bow and placed a hand on the handle of his dagger.

"We don't know you," he said menacingly. "But let me guess."

He looked sharply at Eric's locks of fair hair.

"A Viking if ever I saw one!" the man growled. "Go on. Deny it. I bet you don't even understand what I'm saying."

His companion snorted.

"We've seen his sort before," he said. "Viking raiders who lose their ship. Then end up getting washed-up on the shore."

He grinned mercilessly.

"They don't last long around here," he went on. "Saxons don't like Vikings!"

Eric's heart pounded. He stayed silent and did not know where to turn.

"Say something," the first men sneered. "You don't speak a word of our language."

The Viking boy fought for control.

"I'm on my own," he said, nervously. "I'm doing no harm."

The Saxon hunters were stunned.

"He speaks!" said one. "But not like we do. He's from the North."

Eric seized his chance.

"That's right," he answered quickly. "From beyond the hills. We were fishing and a storm blew up. The boat ran onto the rocks. I'm the only survivor."

The two men looked at each other. They did not believe him.

"Strange accent," said one. "I never heard anyone talk like that before. If you'd been fishing out at sea why did you have a bear cub on board?"

This stumped Eric, desperate for an answer.

"I came across it in the forest, yesterday," he said. "I was cutting branches for my shelter. The cub seemed lost, he added lamely.

The bowman narrowed his eyes. A mean smile spread across his face.

"That bear," he said, "would make nice little fur coats for my kids. Keep them warm in the Winter!"

He trained his arrow on Beowulf and began to pull back the string.

"One shot should do it!"

Eric leapt forward.

"Stop!" he cried. "Leave my cub alone!"

Too late. The arrow flew straight and true towards the defenceless bear. Eric screamed and hurled himself at the hunter. They hit the ground and rolled over in the dirt. The man struck out, landing a heavy blow on the side of the boy's head. Eric lay gasping as the man got up to check his shot. He cursed.

"I missed!"

Beowulf snarled as the fellow pulled a second arrow from his quiver.

"How could I fail from close range?"

Eric shook his bruised head. The bear was alive.

"You didn't miss," said the second Saxon. "The arrow went straight through the bear and didn't leave a mark. I saw it with my own eyes."

An angry Beowulf advanced on the man who had tried to murder him.

"It's magic!" shouted his companion. "The boy's a wizard. Run!"

The two cowards turned and fled. Eric struggled to his feet as they escaped through the trees.

"Are you all right, bear?"

Beowulf stopped growling and settled down. His master ran his hands over his fur searching for a wound. But there was no sign of injury.

"It passed through you?" Eric mused. "That makes you very special."

The cub nosed his master before wandering away to explore the estuary. Swirls of muddy water streamed into the channels as the tide crept in. Eric was content to watch from a distance as Beowulf splashed about, poking under floating strands of seaweed.

"I'd better start a fire," Eric thought. "Those men aren't likely to come back in a hurry. I'll do a little fishing. Then try to think out the future. Do I hang on here or move?"

In truth, he had no idea. But he need not have worried about fishing. Beowulf charged back with a big catch in his mouth. It struggled for freedom, thrashing its silver tail. The bear deposited his prize at Eric's feet.

"A salmon? Thanks, Beowulf. We'll go halves!"

He picked up a sturdy stick and struck the fish's head.

"Now it's out of its misery."

The salmon lay still and Eric got out his knife to gut it.

"These are the bits you like!"

He tossed the fish's guts over to Beowulf.

"And you can have the head and tail!"

Fixing the remains of the salmon on the spit, Eric looked forward to a fine supper provided by the bear. When he came to taste the fish it was smoked to perfection. Beowulf hung around expecting more. He was just as interested as Eric in the pink, muscle flesh. The two travellers settled back to enjoy the night. Beowulf made a final trip to the forest where he rooted for bulbs and beetles. His young master lay back on the ground. It seemed he had not a care in the world. But it was not so. As darkness fell around him, his mind flashed back to his friends. He could not face thinking he was banned from them, forever.

The flames leapt as Eric tossed on a couple of dead branches. It was as though the heat kept up his spirits. He gazed into the night sky where the first stars shone as pinpoints of light.

"I'll imagine the brightest are my friends," he thought. "With Astrid brightest of all!"

His eyelids felt heavy. An owl, out for the night, screeched amongst the trees.

Suddenly, a rapid movement brought Eric to his senses. It was impossible to know what it was. He sat up straight, peering into the near blackness. A fleeting shadow. A rumbling snarl. It was certainly not Beowulf.

"Who's that?" the boy cried out.

His heart raced and he grabbed a burning branch from the fire. Something dark and menacing was out there. A flicker of movement, but no more. First in front, then behind. Eric whirled around with the flaming torch. It was the only weapon to hand.

Again, the threatening snarl. He began to panic, turning one way, then the other. Shadows played tricks in the flames, conjuring up shapes of devils and demons.

"Grrrrrr! Grrrrrrr!"

An electrifying snarl. An enormous beast leapt into the space between Eric and the fire. A black silhouette standing out against the light. Glistening fangs; eyes glowing like hot coals. Forcing the boy to step back in terror.

"Oh no!" he moaned. "The Shuck!"

The beast widened its jaws running with saliva. Eric stared down its throat, the long tongue lolling out of the side of the mouth. Rooted to the spot, he felt weak and helpless. The Shuck raised its head and howled into the night. The outcast froze, dropping the torch which broke into pieces on the ground. The Shuck inched forward. No amount of Wizard's potion could save its next victim. The boy gulped. He smelt its evil breath.

The next moment, Eric was bowled off his feet as something heavy and powerful cannoned into him. The Shuck stopped in its tracks. Beowulf the bear raised himself onto his hind legs. Unbelievably, he towered over Eric. With one mighty swipe of his paw, he cuffed The Shuck across the head. With the other paw, claws outstretched, he struck out and sent the Demon Dog sprawling into the fire. Its anguished howls echoed across the estuary.

As Eric regained his senses, he made out the burning shape of The Shuck in the flames. They sparked and crackled with a new intensity. He covered his eyes. When he dared open them, The Shuck was no more than a pile of ashes. A giant of a bear stood at his side. It dropped down onto all fours before growing smaller by the second.

Beowulf looked up at his master seeking to be petted. Eric knelt and buried his face in the fur. The young Viking rocked back and forth, circling the bear cub with his arms.

"I knew you were special," he sobbed. "What kind of bear are you?"

The cub wriggled out of his master's grip and pounced on a chunk of left-over salmon.

"You deserve that," Eric laughed happily. "You can have all the salmon in the world!"

He wiped his tears and fondled the cub's muzzle.

"You're small again," he said. "But you weren't when you took on The Shuck. You were enormous. The Wizard of the forest promised you would protect me!"

* * * *

CHAPTER NINE

Lief's Smart Plan

Life in the Saxon village went on. Blacksmiths slaved over hot furnaces shaping melted iron into tools or weapons. The freeman tended their animals on small strips of land. And women of all ages worked hard, children running in and out of the dwellings as they swept the floors. Some women fashioned jewellery, sewed, or wove cloth. From dawn to dusk, the community pulled together to make things happen.

Beyond the village, where the river flowed towards the sea, boat-builders repaired their craft. Sounds of hammering and sawing filled the air. In only a few weeks, the young Vikings produced two sleek vessels to rise to the sea's challenge. Chief Alfred was pleased with the progress. But he did not know how unhappy the immigrants were. However hard Vimp and Lief tried to lift spirits, they had little impact. The girls, in particular, were very down. But they were concerned about Astrid who never smiled. She hardly ate and some mornings refused to leave her hut. Freya fretted for her friend.

"She can't carry on like this. Of course Astrid misses Eric. We all do. But he'll survive."

English Emma was not so sure.

"I'd hate to be kicked out on my own," she said. "I wouldn't last a day."

Deep down, the two girls were worried sick for Big Eric. It was Ingrid who understood Astrid best.

"She can't get him out of her mind," she said. "I've tried talking to her but I can't get through."

Time passed and Lief knew things were no better. Sitting with Vimp in their hut, the two boys got into deep conversation.

"D'you know?" Lief said, "We'll never settle here. We don't really belong. It's not that the Saxons are unreasonable. This just isn't our scene. Maybe we should go back home."

The idea shocked Vimp.

"No, Lief," he said, shaking his head. "This is our big chance. We deserted our own land. This is all we have."

His thoughtful friend bowed his head in the semi-darkness.

"Well, I think we should return," he said firmly. "One or two of the others are thinking this way. I miss my family and the girls miss theirs. Why don't we build a new boat and leave?"

Vimp had no answer. He longed for his family, too, especially his younger brothers. His mind was in turmoil.

"We should talk it out," he suggested. "Have a word with Bjorne. He's sensible. And Freya. If anyone knows what's right, it'll be her."

The days passed but the Viking youngsters grew sadder. One evening, after supper, they met up by the river. The air was still, with clouds of insects hovering over the surface. Freya spoke first.

"The girls got together and agreed," she said. "It won't be easy to return our old village. The leaders might still be furious with us. But it's a risk we have to take."

The group sat down in a circle. Astrid's thoughts turned to Eric. If they left Saxon England, he would be abandoned forever. After the meeting, Lief did not say a word. His mind worked, feverishly. Next morning, he and Vimp met up with Freya.

"You're on your own, Vimp," said Lief. "Everyone's for packing up and going home. I have a plan. It involves Eric but I'm only telling you and Freya. It might just work. Tonight, we should talk to Chief Alfred."

Lief explained his idea. His friends listened, carefully, but Vimp still had doubts.

"If you want to get Alfred on side," he said, "you've got to tell him everything. You're suggesting we only reveal part of your plan. The rest we keep secret – even to Alfred. Surely, that can't be right?"

To his disappointment, Freya sided with Lief.

"I understand," she said. "It's a really smart idea. Why should we tell Alfred everything?"

Vimp remained dubious.

"I need to think about this," he said. "It's a risk. If the plan goes wrong, things could get tricky. The Saxons will go mad!"

It drizzled that day. Boat-building was not much fun but it did give Vimp time to ponder. After supper, he, Lief and Freya visited the Chieftain's great hut. Alfred's family slept in corners behind drawn curtains. He made his Viking visitors welcome.

"I think I know why you're here," he said. "I'm just as unhappy about Eric's punishment as you are. But the villagers are afraid of the brooding forest and its threats. You do understand?"

Vimp nodded.

"Thank you for seeing us," he said. "It's not just what's happened to Eric. We've all tried hard to settle and fit in. But..."

Alfred invited the young Vikings to sit down and asked Vimp to continue.

"Lief's come up with a scheme," Vimp said. "He can explain."

Lief rose from his bench.

"With your permission, Alfred, we'd like to construct our own boat. Make it seaworthy and test it out. Then, when wind and weather are set fair, sail back home. Return to our families. We'd have to beg them to forgive us. We'll always be thankful to you for giving us a chance to settle."

He paused.

"I'm sorry," he went on. "Things simply haven't worked out."

Chief Alfred looked solemn.

"We gave you a home," he said. "You were welcomed and earned respect with hard work. What you say does come as a bit of a shock. Yet," he paused, stroking his greying beard, "perhaps not. Last week, I had people on my back complaining about the barley in the fields. It hasn't grown high and the yield will be down. There'll be barely enough grain for Winter. Yesterday, I had to deal with an angry farmer whose cattle have gone lame. He blamed it on Eric and the curse of The Black Shuck. Now, the whole village seethes with rumour. It could get ugly. The people are turning against you. Blaming your arrival for our misfortunes. The death of the Priest came as a bad blow."

Freya felt scared.

"That was horrible," she said. "We were just as upset. Even though it wasn't his fault, poor Eric was found guilty. You say the villagers are turning against us?"

The Chieftain nodded grimly.

"I fear so," he replied. "Some haven't forgotten the old beliefs. When they can't explain events, they look for easy victims to pick on."

He paused and looked them in the eye.

"For your own safety, it might be better if you did leave. I can't say more, now, as I must speak to the Council."

He rose and showed the youngsters to the door. They returned to their huts, deep in thought. At least Alfred had been good enough to listen. It seemed he understood the Vikings' desire to return. And that would suit the village.

Over the next few days, Vimp and company went about their tasks with heavy hearts. Now and again, they caught a glance of hostility from a passing Saxon. The girls reported that the families they worked for did not seem to trust them anymore. Chief Alfred called the Viking group to see him and warned he had serious news. He did not waste time. It had been decided by a Council vote that the new settlers were to leave, at once. So keen was the village to rid itself of The Shuck's curse, it was agreed the Vikings could take the new boat they had just completed.

"I'm very sorry," he told them finally. "I've no quarrel with you. But it's for the best. We'll see you're stocked for the voyage. You leave by the end of the week."

Vimp and his friends stood, dejected. They left the meeting and shuffled back to their huts. Bjorne and Vimp now understood they would have to be the leaders. Organise the expedition and check out the sea-worthiness of the boat. Freya would take charge of food and clothing and support the girls. She soon realised the problem she had with English Emma. What would she decide? To stay with her own people or leave with her Viking companions? Freya needed to find out.

Meanwhile, Vimp and Bjorne spotted Lief was not around. The gentle Viking who had only ever wanted to be a poet had gone missing. So, too, had Eadbehrt and Leofwine, the brave souls who had helped old Anselm find the Wizard. The villagers were not too worried as they assumed the brothers had gone hunting. But for the Vikings, to lose Lief was a worry; his disappearance a complete mystery. Vimp sought out Freya and was surprised by her cool manner.

"Lief's a clever fellow," she said. "We'll see him again. Mark my word. And remember," she continued, "he didn't tell Alfred the whole of our plan. There's that special little bit he left out. Trust him. He's never let us down."

Freya's words puzzled Vimp. But he trusted Lief whom he knew would come up with something different.

The day arrived. Many Saxon villagers were sad to see the Vikings go. Few believed in the tales of forest spirits. With Chieftain Alfred, they lined up on the river bank to wave the youngsters off. The person they most regretted seeing depart was Emma. She had gone in with her friends who had rescued her from Viking slavery. Now, she bid farewell to her own land to set out on a new voyage. But Emma was more concerned about Lief. Why had he not returned? Was he hurt, or lost, somewhere deep in the forest?

Chief Alfred prepared to give the signal to push the longboat into the water. But as he did so, two strong Saxons appeared on the river bank. Leofwine and Eadbehrt splashed up to their waists to have urgent words with Vimp.

"Go in peace," they told him. "Sail North along the coast and keep a good look-out. A lighted fire will be your sign."

The new vessel slid into the river on the turn of the tide. Bjorne stood at the helm, with Vimp giving orders to the rowers. Huddled against the side, Astrid refused to look up and wave goodbye. Gentle Freya spoke softly to her.

"You've got to trust," she told her. "I can't say more. All will be well."

Soon, the longboat rocked on the turbulent waters where river met ocean. The craft cleared the sandbanks and Vimp struck out for sea.

"There's not much wind, boys," he cried. "You'll have to dig in and row hard. We're going home!"

But first, the longboat ran along the coast. Freya organised the girls to go round with water and bites to eat. Only a light breeze blew and Vimp was relieved. He needed an easy start knowing that bad weather was bound to follow. The afternoon sun blazed down on the unprotected rowers. As evening approached, Emma moved forward and stood at the prow. Its mighty dragon head carved through the swell. Something attracted her attention. Was that smoke? Emma raised her hand and squinted into the bright light.

"Vimp!" she cried. "Fire! A beacon."

The young captain pushed his way forward to join her.

"Where?" he asked. "I don't see it."

Emma pointed. A puff of grey-blue smoke snaked into the sky. Vimp stumbled back through his oarsmen.

"Steer to port!" he ordered Bjorne. "Steady now. We're entering shallow waters."

The longboat glided into a bay protected by two low headlands. A bonfire blazed on the shore.

"Steady now!" Vimp called. "We're about to land."

Emma stared ahead. Two boys raced down the beach. They jumped up and down, arms beating the air. Behind them trundled a small bear. Emma could no longer contain herself.

"Lief! Eric!"

She waved wildly. Further back in the boat, Freya helped Astrid to her feet.

"This is for you," she cried. "Look ahead!"

Astrid wobbled as the boat's hull ground onto the sand. She recognised the dancing figure of the boy she so admired. Ragged and sun-burned Eric, bravest of Vikings, punched the air. Lief, standing by his side, grinned from ear to ear. His master plan had worked. Using Leofwine's and Eadbehrt's forest skills, Lief had managed to track down the outcast.

Beowulf, on the other hand, was unimpressed. He had found a crab but it scuttled off to a hiding place. He padded around, impatiently, as it refused to come out.

* * * *

CHAPTER TEN

Freya Goes Home

With all the friends joined up again, it was time to celebrate. The boys went fishing and returned with mackerel and herrings. English Emma took over the cooking, helped by happy Astrid. Eric took everyone to see his shelter.

"It wouldn't win prizes," he confessed, "but it just about keeps out the wind and rain. Beowulf lies outside, most nights. I think he likes the heat of the fire after the embers die down."

The voyagers were thrilled to see the bear cub had stayed with Eric. They petted him and offered pieces of smoked fish. Out of sight of the others, Lief and Vimp drew Eric to one side.

"You're the one to get us across the sea," they told him. "We've thought about it hard. We're returning to our old village to try and make it up with our parents. It won't be easy. Once the fuss dies down, we can prove we're good boat-builders. They'll back down."

Eric came slowly on side. He took one final look at the strange construction he called home then went down to the boat. Bjorne took the helm, insisting Eric deserved a break. It meant he could sit with Astrid. Beowulf sat with them both, not making much sense of boats. It was not long before Eric wanted to take his turn at an oar.

With a change in wind direction, it was possible to put up the big square sail. This gave the rowers a rest. The longboat picked up speed and powered on. Vimp could not believe his luck. At this rate, the sea crossing might only take a couple of days. Up at the dragon head prow, Lief clung to a rope holding up the mast. He relished the spray breaking into his face. Suddenly, his attention was drawn to something ahead. It was a large object. A rock, perhaps? Sticking out of the sea with waves breaking over it. But it appeared to be moving. Lief called for Vimp to come forward.

"I see it, now," he said. "Dead ahead. Better steer to starboard. Haul up the sail and get ready with the oars."

He caught Bjorne's attention and signalled. Bjorne leaned on the tiller. The boat creaked, taking on the waves at a new angle. Hand over eyes, Vimp squinted into the distance.

"It can't be a rock," he speculated. "Not this far out...'

Lief agreed.

Suddenly, the object disappeared.

"Am I imagining things?" he asked. "Now you see it; now you don't!"

The ship's skipper did not argue. He felt uneasy. To collide with something just under the surface had him worried. The two look-outs scanned the horizon.

"We're going to hit it!"

The thing was back on the surface. Vimp shouted at his helmsman to change course. A plume of spray burst from the mysterious object. Bjorne fought the tiller. Now, even he could see what the fuss was about. A massive greyish lump, lined and wrinkled and nearly away," Astrid implored clamping across the bows. A second explosion of vapour spurted from the object. Up front, Lief and Vimp had the best view. It moved across their course. Tharg scrambled up to join them.

"It's a whale," he cried. "Seriously big!"

He stood up on his toes.

"Did you see that? A second spout! Smaller. There! Over to the left."

The others followed his finger. Emma could not contain her excitement.

"It's a baby. A little behind the big one."

A worrying thought flashed through her mind.

"Will they attack us?"

Tharg laughed.

"I don't think so," he said. "Can we get nearer?"

Vimp was not too sure. With a few more pulls on the oars, the longboat was about to cross the whales' path. But he gave no orders to alter course. When they got close, he told the rowers to turn and take a quick look. The boat slowed and the sailors gazed at a pair of sperm whales, ploughing through the sea.

"Huge head!" Vimp cried. "It takes up about a third of its body."

At that moment, the mother humped close to the surface and let out a thunderous, watery gasp all could hear. A puff of fine spray angled in front of her. The calf kept to her far side, bravely keeping up with its parent. Emma was enchanted.

"I heard whales were all smooth and sloping at the front," she said. "This one's got a head like a massive chunk of rock. Where's the eye?"

"There!"

Lief leapt for joy.

"She's seen us!"

For a fleeting moment, the gentle giant appeared to fix the boat with a look that seemed neither unfriendly or afraid. She swam majestically through the waves making sure her calf was on the side furthest from the onlookers. The rowers rested their oars and watched the ocean giants swim off. The mother dived, lifting her splendid tail before thrashing it down onto the surface. Both she and the calf disappeared from view, only to re-emerge and continue their sea marathon. Vimp wasted no time.

"Start the rowing!"

The boys got back into their stroke and pulled to a rhythm. Still the weather held fair and the boat made progress. It gave Lief time to think. As usual, a cunning plan formed in his mind. He called Vimp and Freya over and asked Tharg to join them.

"With any luck, we may spot the coastline, tomorrow," he said. "Then we'll have to work out which way to turn to find our old river. But I'm still worried about our welcome. We had to escape from the village to save Emma's life. Also, because none of the boys wanted to fight. There'll still be people who'll be mad at us."

He paused.

"So here's my idea."

Lief reminded them that Tharg was not from their village. He was just a stranger they had stumbled across. This meant that no one in the village could get angry with him. Lief suggested the boy from a different community might be very useful.

"I can't force you, Tharg," he said, "but if we land a bit down river and out of sight, you could make first contact with the Chieftain. Find out what kind of reception we might get. Ask if he'd be pleased to see us again. Or be really angry. If the village won't forgive, you could slip away and return to the boat. At least we'd know where we stand."

It was a lot to ask of Tharg but he saw sense in the idea.

"You were good to me when I needed you," he said. "I haven't forgotten. Lief saved my life. Now it's pay-back time."

Tharg felt proud he had been given a special task to do. Freya and Vimp suggested he should think it over, first. But his mind was made up.

"You could be running into danger," he told them. "That would be terrible after what you've been through. So I'm pleased to help."

Lief slapped him over the shoulder.

"We shan't let you go alone, Tharg," he promised. "Three of us will accompany you, most of the way. We can lie up at the forest edge until you get back. Then, one way or the other, we'll know what to do."

Two long nights spent in a rocking boat, far out at sea, was no fun. But the young crew stuck to their task. Early in the afternoon of the third day they sighted land. It was a fantastic moment. Although few admitted it, they had all missed their Viking homes. When they left the village they had defied their parents. Now, returning was giving them problems. They would have to admit their bold adventure had failed.

"I know the coastline well," Tharg told Vimp. "My family fished up and down it. So I should spot a familiar landmark."

Eric was back at the helm.

"We'll head South," Vimp commanded. "Keep an eye out for sandbanks. The look-outs will shout if they spot rocks ahead."

Still the weather held and, by early evening, Tharg guided them to the river outlet they sought. As the sun began to sink over the western horizon, he called Vimp over.

"Those blue hills in the distance. And the mountains beyond. That's where the stream that flows past your village starts."

Vimp looked up into the dark, tree slopes. Three hills. Two humped and rounded and a higher one rising nearly to a point. His heart beat faster. Vimp remembered this view from his earliest days. He could not thank Tharg enough.

"You recognised them before I did. And you're not even from our village."

Tharg smiled. His father and uncle were skilled fishermen and had taught him well. Vimp made up his mind. Summoning Freya and Bjorne, he discussed pulling into the shore where they could anchor for the night. The rowers brought the longboat in close then shipped their oars. The vessel ground into the muddy sand as four or five of the boys leapt overboard with ropes to pull it in. Wading waist deep in the gentle swell, they hauled the boat as high up the shore as it would go.

Lief and Freya jumped off, next. It was their task to organise collecting wood and starting a fire to make a camp for the night.

To be on dry land was magical enough but they felt happy just to be home. It was amusing watching Eric and Freya trying to encourage Beowulf off the boat. At first, the cub did not seem to catch on. But once he scented the distant trees and felt the sand under his paws, he got on message. Keeping his master in sight, he snuffled around, searching for tasty delicacies under rocks, or clumps of seaweed. After supper, the Vikings sat round the fire to enjoy the red glow of the smouldering timbers. The hunched figures of Lief, Vimp, Freya and Tharg sat some way off. As the half-moon rose in the night sky, they planned next day's expedition.

"I'll explain everything to the others before we set out, tomorrow morning," Vimp said. "We'll talk it out between ourselves, for now. The village isn't too far down river. In daylight, we'll find a forest track. Get as near as we can without being spotted. Remember, there'll be guard dogs out with the sheep. I think you know what to do, Tharg?"

The Viking who did not belong to the village nodded, gravely.

"I'll go in on my own," he said. "That won't frighten anyone. And I'll ask to be taken to Chieftain Harald saying I have news of his daughter, Freya. Also the rest of the boys and girls."

Freya listened carefully. She felt unhappy at being left out and was determined to be involved.

"I'm coming with you," she stated plainly.

Lief raised his eyebrows but Freya was not to be argued with.

"I want to talk to my father," she said. "He'll listen to me."

Tharg felt more confident. Going in on his own was not easy so Lief and Vimp finally gave way.

"We'll tell Freya's father," said Tharg, "that our longboat's landed some distance away. And that everyone wants to return to the village. But only if none of the crew, Vimp especially, isn't punished for deserting."

Vimp smiled ruefully.

The Chieftain's daughter tried to hide her excitement. She loved her parents and wondered about her grandmother. Was she even alive? And what about her brothers and sisters? Freya could not wait to see them again.

"My father will be fine," she said. "I can twist him round my little finger!"

Lief was not so sure.

"Listen," he said. "I don't want to be a spoiler. Things could go wrong. So what happens then?"

Tharg had given the matter some thought.

"That's the tricky bit," he agreed. "If things don't work out, Freya and I will have to get back to you to give the warning. We'll make a run for it. They won't know which way. We've trekked through the forest so it'll take them time to work out where our boat is. We can push off before they launch a raider."

Vimp felt concerned as he knew how good the raider rowers were.

"We might get a head start but they have much faster boats. We'll have to row for our lives!"

Freya protested.

"It's not going to be like that!" she scorned. "It'll work out. Trust me!"

They got up and re-joined the others before settling down beneath the stars, to grab a few hours' sleep.

Next day, dawned bright and clear. First, there were boat repairs to carry out. Some of the planking had leaked so gaps were stuffed with coarse hair. A fishing party put out lines, with Bjorne and Eric taking command on the shore. Late in the afternoon, Vimp, Lief, Freya and Tharg set out on their crucial mission.

"Good luck!" Eric wished them. "We'll have the boat ready to sail the moment you need it. But it shouldn't come to that."

He, too, was thinking of his family and longed to see them. The small party set off and waved back when they reached the trees. It was not long before they discovered a hunting track that led to their birth village. The path was overgrown so they selected stout branches and beat down the brambles.

The pungent scent of wood fires told the adventurers they were getting close. They hid in the trees to survey the huts, clustered by the river. Vimp could hardly contain himself. He spotted his family home and thought of the folks, inside.

Only Tharg had never previously set eyes on the scene before them. Nearer, were the fields where farmers grazed their animals. Cows munched contentedly at the lush grass and pigs snuffled under the trees. Vimp knew there was no time to waste.

"We'll watch you all the way," he said. "Be brave. Don't let anyone push you around. We must make a deal with our people. We can't fail."

He and Lief stood in the shadows as Tharg and Freya set out across the open meadow. The livestock took little notice as they approached the wooden defence gate. A villager stepped forward to challenge them. It was too far away to hear what he shouted.

If Tharg was nervous, Freya's pulse was racing. Everything was so familiar. It was almost as if she had never been away.

"Halt, strangers! Show yourselves."

A rough voice demanded to know who they were. Tharg took a deep breath.

"We come in peace," he said. "My name is Tharg. I live along the coast. Our Chieftain sends you greetings."

A fair-bearded man stood in their way. He showed no hint of friendliness.

"That may be so," he said, suspiciously. "We don't welcome newcomers."

He looked curiously at Freya.

"Do I know you?" he asked. "I've seen you before."

The young girl smiled, shyly, and looked him in the eye.

"You should know me," she told the man. "I'm Freya, eldest daughter of Chieftain Harald. Take me to him. I've not seen my father for some time."

The guard called over to two other men, repairing a nearby hut. They put down their tools and strolled across. Neither smiled and Freya did not recognise them. The first man winked at his companions.

"Young lady says she's the former Chieftain's daughter. A likely story. If it's true she wouldn't bother coming here. Not after what happened."

He leered, unpleasantly.

"Well," said the man. "We've got news for you, miss. Your so-called father is no longer around. He got captured by us Norsemen. We stuffed half your people into boats. We heard one was lost at sea. No survivors. So, this village is in our hands, now. There's not too many old inhabitants left."

Freya stood dumbfounded. Had her family been drowned? One of the hut-repairers stepped forward.

"We need new slaves to re-build the village," he sneered. "These two will fit the bill, nicely."

He lunged forward and grabbed Tharg by his tunic. The boy wriggled free but was easily over-powered.

"Take them along to the new Chief," the first man commanded. "This way!"

He shoved them forward. There was no point in struggling. Freya and Tharg were marched to a small hut and forced inside. They groped in the dark as a bar clamped across the door. As far as they could make out the hut was bare. No furniture; nothing to sit on except the earth floor. Outside, the men discussed what to do next.

It was a total disaster. Lief's plan for the young Vikings to return safely to their families had been ripped in pieces.

* * * *

CHAPTER ELEVEN

Hugi And Thialfi

On the edge of the wood, Lief and Vimp felt nervous. Had something gone wrong? Perhaps Freya and Tharg had been asked to stay the night. But it was impossible to work out why no message had been sent to them. As daylight faded they began to fear the worst. They could not stay in the forest but were afraid to move down to the village. It was now too late to get back to the longboat. In the deepening shadows, Vimp thought he detected a slight movement. Something, or someone, ghosted past.

"Lief," he whispered. "We're not alone!"

His friend needed no telling. He, too, had spotted something stir. Were they were being surrounded? Vimp peered across the meadow in the gathering gloom. A grey shadow slipped past. Then another. His heart missed a beat.

"Not people," he hissed. "Wolves!"

Lief shuddered. He had heard tales of children being taken from villages, at night. It hardly seemed possible. Now, he was not so sure.

"Where are they going?" he whispered.

It seemed as though the wolves were not interested in the human intruders. The boys watched as a tight hunting pack sneaked across the field. Heads lowered; shoulders hunched. The grey predators slunk towards the animal stockade.

"They're going for the sheep pens," said Vimp. "But the walls are too high."

"Not if those wolves are hungry," Lief replied. "They'll create chaos in there."

Unaware of the threat, the villagers settled for the night. Freya, imprisoned in her hut, was startled by the sudden opening of the door. Men with flaming torches crowded round. A fierce-looking ruffian spoke in an accent not easy to understand.

"Chief Einar sends us," he told the frightened pair. "He expects answers and it's our job to get them."

He took a step forward.

"Don't try anything clever. Especially that one!"

The brute pointed at Freya.

"We know about you."

His companions followed him in.

"Tell us," he went on, "where you're from. Where's your boat? How many fighting men do you have?"

His eyes smouldered in the light of the flickering flames. Tharg struggled to his feet to protect Freya.

"We come in peace," he stuttered. "You can see we're no threat. Since you know about Freya, you'll know she escaped from this village. We're just kids. Not fighters."

The man coughed with scorn.

"A likely story! You've been sent to report on us. Check out our defences. It's a trick –but we haven't fallen for it. You planned to get back to your comrades and tell them we're a pushover."

Freya got up, anger rising.

"Tharg speaks the truth," she told the alien men. "We're just a boatload of boys and girls. That's all."

She folded her arms and tried to look defiant. One of the men spoke up from the back.

"Boys and girls, eh? This place needs new slaves. We could sell them on. Young slaves are worth their weight in gold!"

Immediately, Freya realised her mistake. The leading man seized the advantage.

"A boatload of kids, eh? As Sigurd rightly points out, you could be worth a fortune if we trade you on."

He lunged at Tharg and grabbed him by the throat.

"Tell us where your boat is. If you don't, we'll take your little friend away. She'll soon cough up."

Tharg felt the cold point of steel beneath his chin. He had to tell. There was no choice. But before he had the chance there was a commotion at the door. An hysterical woman ran in, screaming.

"Wolves! They're amongst the sheep. Hurry!"

The leader hesitated then ordered the men out.

"Don't dare move!" he called back to his prisoners.

Freya heard raised shouts above the bleatings of panicking sheep. People rushed to the scene with weapons and fire torches. She and Tharg stood rooted to the spot. A sinister shadow fell across the open door, followed by another. Two large wolves stood framed at the entrance. Tharg shrank back, pulling Freya with him.

"Fear not, my friends! We're not here to harm you. Freya knows who we are."

Tharg nearly fainted. Was he going mad?

"Follow us," the leading wolf demanded. There's no time for delay."

Freya shook herself free of Tharg's iron grip.

"Hugi! Thialfi!"

She threw herself forward and buried her arms in the wolves' thick fur.

Tharg stood open-mouthed. Freya laughed with joy.

"They saved my life! Hugi and Thialfi, brothers of Agnar, the great, grey wolf."

She buried her face into Thialfi's fur.

"What are you doing here? How did you know?"

Thialfi wasted no time on explanations.

"Come!" he ordered. "We must hurry!"

He sprang out of the hut with the two escapers, close behind. Brother Hugi brought up the rear as they raced for the outer fence. Thialfi scrambled over whilst Freya and Tharg clambered over the top. Freya fell heavily. Tharg dragged her to her feet.

"Run!" he implored.

Hugi padded alongside to keep her going.

Out at the treeline, Vimp and Lief watched in bewilderment. Bright flames lit up the scene and angry voices rang across the meadow. Swift, wolfine shadows snaked back into the wood. Two human figures followed, one struggling to keep up. Vimp ran out of his hiding place to aid Freya. He was astonished to find two fine wolves at her side.

"Hugi…is it you? And Thialfi?"

Tharg interrupted.

"Don't delay! They'll pursue. To the boat!"

It was easier said than done. The deeper they headed into the wood, the greater the gloom.

Hugi and Thialfi took the lead, using their excellent night vision. As they fled, Vimp was aware of quiet footsteps, padding behind. The whole pack was with them.

"Torches!"

Lief spotted dancing lights threading between the trees. By now, Freya limped badly but he urged her on.

"Vimp! Get ahead with Thialfi. Tell Eric to make ready. Half the village is after us!"

The Viking boy and wolf increased their pace. It seemed as though Thialfi knew exactly where the longboat had landed. Reaching the edge of the wood, they saw its dark silhouette in the moonlight. Vimp raced to the beach and alerted the waiting crew. Bjorne immediately organised the rowers, ordering the girls to climb on board.

"We're not leaving without Freya!" Ingrid shouted.

She lit a torch and ran towards trees. Eric and Astrid chased after her to discover Freya hobbling towards them.

"I can't go any further!"

She crumpled into a heap. Eric saw her ankle was black and swollen. He bent down and lifted her in his arms.

"We'll make it!" he promised and lumbered back to the beach with his precious burden.

Angry shouts went up and he spotted the leading torches through the trees. As Eric broke out of the wood, the longboat was already half afloat, oarsmen crouching at their benches. The big Viking boy splashed into the water and pushed Freya into the waiting arms of Vimp and Bjorne.

"Jump aboard, Eric. You're last!" Vimp yelled as they heaved their friend over the gunwhale.

The longboat slid across the silvery surface of the estuary. Two proud wolves stood at the water's edge and howled their farewells into the night. Freya struggled to her feet, tears freely spilling down her cheeks. The rescuers saluted the wolf brothers until a dark cloud passed over the moon.

Hugi and Thialfi could not hang about. They turned away, satisfied with their evening's work. The pack followed, keen to escape the men with torches. Morning would bring its revenge when the pursuers would set out again with weapons and hounds.

Curiously, not one sheep or lamb had been harmed.

* * * *

CHAPTER TWELVE

An Odd Fish

"Loosen the sail!"

Two of the oarsmen, backed up by Lief and Vimp, leapt forward to open the great square sheet. The sail flapped loudly in the rising wind. Eric watched from the helm where he had taken over. He was bothered about the chance that the alien Vikings were in pursuit.

"Are we doing the right thing?" he called. "They'll see the sail in the moonlight and run us down. We can't outpace them."

Vimp insisted it was best.

"We've got time to get clear before they can set off. And they'll have to navigate the river. Tricky in the dark. If we use this wind we'll get away with it."

Meanwhile, the rowers put their backs into the work. The craft cut through the waves in the freshening breeze. Black clouds obscured the moon, making both longboat and sail harder to see. Back at the helm, Eric was more worried about the rise in the wind. It was great for escaping, but troublesome if it increased. He looked at the fleecy clouds racing across the sky. The further the vessel sailed out, the larger the waves.

The crew rowed in near darkness. Only now and again did Eric get a glimpse of the Pole Star needed to stay on course.

Glancing over his shoulder, he hoped the Norsemen had not risked setting out. Vimp made his way, aft.

"I think we're safe," he said.

His helmsman grew more concerned about the wind.

"We should furl the sail," Eric urged. "Hoist it back up and make secure. There's a stiff breeze blowing behind us. And I don't know what the tide's doing. If it's moving in the opposite direction, things could get dicey."

The ship rolled, making the point.

"We're losing control," he went on, fighting the sea thrusting against the rudder. "It's cutting up rough. We'll have to ride out the storm."

Vimp knew Eric spoke sense.

"I'll order the sail up," he shouted, grasping onto a stay as the longboat pitched and rolled.

"Sooner the better!"

Vimp lurched forward to organise the urgent task. Now, only the rowers powered the boat. Dimly, in brief moments of moonlight, Vimp saw the longboat's dragonhead rise and fall. Ahead, he spotted an enormous swell. The creaking boat climbed it, trembled at the crest, and crashed down the other side. A cloud of cold spray burst over the prow, drenching the crew. Two of the rowers tumbled from their benches and lost their oars. Wind whistled through the rigging. Eric was right. A storm was brewing.

As the craft rose to the top of the next wave, it shuddered and pitched sideways. The tiller tore out of Eric's hand. Lief spotted the danger and grabbed it to force the boat back on course. Huddled against the sides, the girls clung on to each other. In previous times, Freya might have used her strange powers to summon aid from the Gods. Now, she was no more than a frightened human being. Up at the mast, Vimp saw the dragon rise to take on the next wave. For a split second, the boat perched on top of the crest before plunging down. The dragon's neck snapped off to be whisked away in the foam.

"Slow the boat down!" Eric yelled into the wailing wind. "Get forward and bundle up the spare oars. Tie them together. Secure the rope then cast them over the stern. The weight will help drag us back."

Lief splashed forward. He was astonished at the amount of water the boat had shipped. Vimp put all hands to work, baling over the gunwhales. With Bjorne and Tharg's help, he tied up the spare oars and hitched the end of the rope to a spar. Then they dropped it over the stern.

"The spare sail!" Lief shouted at Bjorne. "Chuck it overboard. Secure the rope first!"

They pulled the emergency sail bundled under the rowing benches.

"Make it tight!"

With an enormous heave, the boys pushed the massive weight over the back. The sail sank like an anchor and the boat responded. The two weights prevented it from tipping over the tops of the waves to smash down into the next.

With the dawn, the awful storm showed signs of blowing out. Virtually everyone had been seasick but knew they had ridden out the gale. As the sky cleared, calmer waters lay ahead. The crew was dismayed to discover the loss of the dragon head. A jagged spar stuck up where it had once braved the waves. The ship was water-logged; oars broken or lost. But they recovered the spares thrown overboard. As for the second sail, it had to be abandoned. No-one had the strength to pull it in.

The longboat wallowed on the calmer swell of the waves and Lief roused his rowers for a final effort. Eric was released from the helm to be replaced by Bjorne. He collapsed over a rowing bench and dropped into a deep sleep. Once more, the helmsman's courage had matched whatever had been thrown at him. Astrid stayed at his side whilst the soaked bear cub nuzzled his master's back.

Lief slapped Vimp over the shoulder.

"We made it!" he said. "You saved your ship."

Vimp was too exhausted to smile but his spirits were suddenly raised by a call from the look-out.

"Land ahead!"

What lay before them was not especially inviting. The longboat approached a line of low sea cliffs. The beach was narrow and the sailors feared hazardous rocks might guard the shoreline. They were in luck, however, and the craft beached safely. Some of the boys leapt overboard to pull it in.

"I've an idea where we are," Vimp told Lief.

"I can't be sure," he went on, "but that gale was a South-Easterly. You're not going to believe this. I think we're back on the island of the Saxons. Just a lot further North."

He ran his hands through his dripping hair.

"We've been blown way off course."

He studied the forbidding cliffs.

"I think we've been carried up the coast. Maybe to the land of the Picts."

Lief gave him a funny look.

"Picts?" he asked. "They're supposed to be really fierce. We'll have to keep watch."

Bjorne struggled to light a fire on the beach. He had managed to keep his flints but it was hard to find tinder wood. With help from the girls, he found bits and pieces and made a cheering blaze. Water and rations were shared around. Bread and hard cheese had never tasted better. As for Beowulf, he nosed around scratching under piles of seaweed for anything to satisfy his ravenous hunger.

Over the next two days, the crew repaired the boat that had sprung numerous leaks. But they could not replace the dragon. Vimp, Lief and Freya planned what to do next. Fortunately, the weather improved, allowing for a bit of exploration. Bjorne and Tharg struggled along shore tugging something behind them.

"We found a shipwreck!" they cried. "A fighting boat packed full of stuff. Except it's got soaked. Tools, weapons, bales of cloth. All the food's perished but there's gold and jewellery on board. The raiders must have stolen it. We think all the crew drowned."

Bjorne spread out a net discovered in the wreck.

"See this!" he said, as his friends crowded around. "For fishing - just what we need. Trail it behind the boat and we can catch mackerel!"

Vimp jumped for joy.

"Show us!" he commanded.

The others needed no bidding and ran along the shore after Bjorne and Tharg. Rounding a small clump of rocks, they discovered the broken hull of a Viking raider. They waded out to explore every inch. The washed-up goods were no longer any use to a dead crew. Eric was impressed by an array of axes, mallets and other building tools. It seemed as though the raiders might have been searching for somewhere to settle.

It was time to go to sea, again. Vimp and Freya decided the group had to find a gently-sloping coastline with a sheltered landing beach. And, hopefully, trees to provide timbers for buildings. Lief still had his doubts.

"The farther North we travel," he said, "the fewer trees we see. The ones that do manage are half-sized and battered by the winds. My guess is we'll have to learn to build huts from stone. There are plenty of rocks scattered around. I expect Winter, up here, is really fierce. The winds would blow wooden buildings down."

Vimp listened carefully. No-one knew how to erect stone dwellings. Two days later, the boat was ready to put out, and the sea calmer. The rowers kept close to the shore fearing they might get lost in a vast ocean. Each night, the longboat headed back to the land so the crew could find harbour and make a fire. Smoked fish headed the menu and the happiest eater was the young bear. Beowulf had adjusted to life at sea as long as he could keep with Eric or Astrid. With the others he was slightly grumpy, behaving more like a normal bear.

The longboat cruised up the coast giving Bjorne a chance to try his fishing skills. With Tharg's help, he thrust the new net over the stern. To delight of both boys, they netted their first catch.

"Throw the little ones back," Bjorne urged. "We'll never eat them so let them grow up."

When he hauled the next load aboard, he was in for an almighty surprise. Captured with the sleek, shining mackerel was the oddest fish he had ever seen. It lay gasping at the bottom of the net. The head was large and bulbous and enormous eyes looked up, mournfully, from the deck. Bjorne pointed it out to Tharg. Although Tharg's family were all fishermen, he had never come across such a sea creature. He glanced at Bjorne who appeared just as puzzled. Tharg broke the silence and asked the obvious question.

"Is that a fish or a human? I've heard folks tell of mermaids after they've returned from voyages. But this one's different!"

Bjorne bent low and slipped his hands beneath the scaly catch and lifted it. His eyes nearly popped out. This was no mermaid. It certainly did not have the face of a beautiful young maiden, nor the flowing hair. Further, the creature possessed no tail yet, with head and fins, it looked extremely fishy.

"Am I imagining things?" Tharg asked Bjorne. "It has a fish head…'

His voice tailed off and Bjorne attempted to finish his sentence.

"And sort of …'

Bjorne blinked and looked again. The fish, if that was what it was, possessed spindly-looking fins and legs. Bjorne held the unhappy creature in his hands as everyone crowded round. No-one spoke. It was the fish creature that broke the long silence.

"Please don't harm me!"

A speaking fish?

"I need water. I can't breathe without it. Don't throw me back in the sea. My left leg's agony. It got caught in your net. I'll never be able to swim again. Not that my pitiful legs were ever any use. At least, that's what my wife says. She calls me a good-for-nothing-waste-of-time. It's hardly my fault I'm hopeless!"

A big salty tear rolled out from one eye. Recovering from its shock, the creature looked round, pleadingly, at its captors. By now, Freya and Vimp had joined the interested crowd. The girl who had once possessed extraordinary powers over wild animals spoke gently to the little fish person.

"I think I know what you are," she said. "Don't be afraid. We'll look after you."

Freya stood up and asked Bjorne to lift over an empty water barrel.

"Fill it with sea water. Quick as you can!"

With Tharg's help, the barrel was soon half full. Bjorne carried the fishman and dipped it in. It dived for a few seconds before breaking the surface.

"So kind," it murmured. "So very kind. I can't tell you how grateful I am."

Freya tried hard not to laugh. Her fishy guest was curiously polite.

"I don't breathe air, you know. I use gills. Not like my wife. She breathes too much and never stops talking. You'll excuse me?"

It dived back down into the water before struggling back to the surface. It was an extraordinary sight, holding its head above water and flapping its tiny fins. Freya spotted Beowulf was showing sudden interest. The bear's eagerness for a tasty bite of fish was well known.

"No you don't, Beowulf!" Freya scolded the cub who was about to dip his paw into the barrel.

The fishman dived out of harm's way as Freya pushed Beowulf off and ordered him back to his place. The next time the fishman appeared, it stuck only half its head out, looking anxious.

"Don't worry," Freya said, comfortingly. "We'll keep an eye on the bear. Beowulf won't harm you!"

The fishman popped its head out a little further.

"Most grateful. You must call me Murrough," he said. "That's what all we mermen are called. A foolish bunch. No good for anything. Excuse me!"

Again, the Murrough disappeared before re-emerging. Dripping and spluttering, he fixed Freya with his big eye.

"You wouldn't have a nice strand of seaweed, by any chance? So tasty. I can never get enough of it!"

Freya searched through the net and retrieved a few bits and pieces. She fished them out and offered them to the Murrough. But he had dived deep in his barrel, again, fixing oxygen into his gills. He splashed up.

"Ah! There you are."

By now, half a dozen curious faces were staring into his new watery world. The Murrough was providing excellent entertainment. He grasped the slimy seaweed in his tiny fins and crammed it into his mouth.

"Mmm…Lovely!" he said. "Any more?"

As the crew fed him with delicious morsels, he grew even more talkative. It seemed he had swum out from a rock pool he shared with his wife. Carried off by a strong current, the Murrough had found it impossible to turn back.

"I panicked at first," he told his enchanted audience. "Then I had a marvellous thought. I was out of range of my wife. You wouldn't want to meet her. She's dreadful!"

Requiring a further oxygen fix, he upturned before returning to the top.

"Now, where was I? Oh, yes! Mrs Murrough. My wife. All sweet looks and wet smiles. But don't you believe it. She'd have you under the sea in a twinkling!"

Granting the Murrough a few more seconds for his next dive, Lief questioned him even closer.

"You mean your wife's a mermaid?" he said. "They're legends. Relaxing in the sun and gazing into mirrors. Combing their long hair. I've heard they sing and lure sailors to run their boats onto rocks. Is that true?"

The Murrough sighed.

"Mermaids look all innocent," he said. "But they're not to be trusted. Believe me. Don't go near them. That's where I went wrong. A big mistake. If you take my advice, steer clear of mermaids. Now, if you'll excuse me, I need a rest. See you in the morning!"

With a final splash, the little merman up-ended. His admirers caught a glimpse of his pathetically frail human legs. Beowulf was fascinated by the new arrival and understood every word. The cub had decided to make a friend of the Murrough. He would guard the barrel against all intruders, especially mermaid wives!

* * * *

CHAPTER THIRTEEN

Morag's Song

"Hello!"

Beowulf stared over the top of the barrel as the Murrough broke surface. The merman gulped, wide-eyed, before realising the bear meant no harm.

"Ah, hello!"

The two creatures looked each other with curiosity.

"I thought you were a fish," said Beowulf. "You certainly look like one."

The Murrough paused for thought.

"I suppose I do," he replied. "But only half a fish, actually. You promise you won't eat me?"

Before the bear had time to reply, the Murrough dipped under the surface. He returned for more conversation.

"I don't suppose these humans take me seriously," he said. "Who does?"

Beowulf thought hard.

"We're in the same boat," he said.

It was quite a good joke for a bear.

"They're a good lot and Eric Bignose rescued me. They think I'm simple and don't know I'm intelligent. I keep it to myself, of course, but I understand every word they speak."

The Murrough looked serious in his fish-like way.

"Very wise! You never know when that can come in handy."

For the rest of the morning, as the craft sailed along the coast of the Picts, Beowulf and the Murrough enjoyed each other's company. The bear got used to his new friend's plunges under water.

"I can swim a bit," the bear said. "I like splashing in pools and diving. It's dark, deep down, isn't it?"

"Hard to port!"

A shout went up from Vimp standing at the broken prow with no dragon.

"The coast's turning West. We should follow!"

Back at the helm, Eric did as ordered. The longboat hit a rough patch of water. Eric was glad Astrid had joined him.

"What's Beowulf up to?" he asked.

Astrid tossed her hair and laughed.

"He's best friends with that incredible Murrough," she said. "Which is nice. After all, bears can't communicate with us."

Eric felt strong vibrations run up the rudder, making his hands shake.

"What's this tide doing?" he wondered, peering over the side. "It's racing past. The wind's one way and tide the other. I don't understand."

Neither did Astrid. She left that sort of thing to the sailors. The craft began to bucket up and down. Although the waves were not large, they were choppy. Eric clung on to the tiller for grim death.

"I can't control it," he shouted. "Call Vimp!"

But Vimp needed little telling. He had already seen the rushing waters, up ahead. It seemed the currents were running in different directions. He turned and waved to his helmsman.

"Go left!" he yelled. "Steer away from this rough water."

Try as he might, Eric kept fighting the rudder. Vimp pleaded with the oarsmen to pull harder, on the starboard side. But the boat failed to respond. It rocked precariously in waters that swirled in all directions. Dead ahead, there seemed to be a deep hole in the sea.

"Keep steering left!"

There was not time to look back and watch Eric losing the battle. The vessel was being sucked towards the forbidding hole of circling, black water. Vimp had heard about whirlpools. Now he stared one in the face. As he did so, a hideous figure emerged from the centre where the water spiralled down. It had the head of a wild woman; long strands of untidy hair dripping over her bony shoulders. She grinned wickedly, showing large gaps between blackened teeth. The sea witch cackled over the roar of the waters threatening to engulf the boat.

"I have you in my power. No-one escapes the clutches of Old Morag!"

Vimp looked helplessly on as the craft circled to its doom. The witch sang in a grating voice.

"Sweery, sweery, linkum-loo! Do to them as I now do."

With a supreme effort, the little Murrough leapt out of his barrel and flopped on the deck. Half stunned, he crawled between the legs of the shaken rowers. Then he wriggled his way up to the prow. Vimp glanced down. The Murrough waved his puny hands.

"Throw things into her pool," he urged. "Barrels, oars, crates…Morag loves possessions."

As the sea witch sang her song, again, Vimp came to his senses. The boat was about to drawn into her lair.

"Chuck anything in," Vimp shouted. "Barrels…oars… weapons! You others… row for your lives!"

A barrage of goods and belongings cascaded over the gunwhale. Old Morag broke off her song.

"Thank you! Thank you!" she screeched. "All for me. Where's my net?"

She busied herself collecting new trophies as the longboat broke away from the pool's magnetic pull. Soon, the waters calmed allowing the rowers to pick up a steadier rhythm. Vimp looked down at the Murrough who had saved them. He lay gasping on the deck, eyes clouding over. The young captain saw the little merman was close to death. He knelt and picked him up. Then he hurried back to the water barrel. He dipped the Murrough in the brine, holding his gills just under the surface. Very slowly, signs of life returned. The merman's head twitched and he rolled one eye. Freya joined Vimp at the barrel. She touched the Murrough's scaly face and spoke lovingly to him.

"You said you were useless," she said. "I didn't believe that at the time. Now, I know for certain. Mr Murrough... you're a star!"

Vimp smiled and let the Murrough slide gently into the water. The two friends stayed by the barrel to see the strange little merman recover. Beowulf lumbered up to join them. He raised himself on hind legs and peered in. His new friend swam slowly around the bottom, preferring to keep himself to himself. The Murrough felt unable to cope with fame or gratitude.

Vimp shuddered. He had been the one who stared into the treacherous depths of the whirlpool. The voyage was becoming a nightmare; disaster following disaster. How long would it go on like this? The crew had lost over half its goods and provisions. Everyone was exhausted and swiftly losing heart.

"What's next?" Vimp wondered.

He kept the question to himself although he knew Freya read his mind. He thrust his head in his hands and began to cry. His brave shoulders shook as he sobbed. Freya took Vimp in her arms to give him time. She threw Lief a knowing look as he made sure the rowers kept to their stroke. And Eric, who had also seen what was happening, made way at the helm for Bjorne. He moved forward to kneel by his friend's side.

"Cry as much as you want, Vimp," he said. "Just let it go. You're the one who's got us this far. And we're not finished yet. We'll reach our destination - wherever it may be."

He ruffled his pal's tousled hair and moved off to join Astrid who organised the next round of rations. Freya gave Vimp a hug and rocked him, softly, like a child.

"Eric's right," she whispered, hoarsely. "Don't despair. Without you, we'd have perished long ago. There's a big inlet, ahead, where we'll find shelter for the night. Remember, Vimp, tomorrow's another day. The sun will rise and we'll all be warmed by its rays."

Freya knew she needed to take more care of the boy who had come to her rescue. The young longboat captain was at the end of his tether and needed a break. But Freya was confident the others would rally round and do their duty: Eric; Lief; Bjorne; Tharg; Astrid; Ingrid and English Emma. She sensed they were nearing the end of the long journey. Something deep inside told her all would be well.

Freya could not have been more wrong. The great voyage was not finished. Far more challenging hazards lurked just around the corner.

* * * *

CHAPTER FOURTEEN

Battle Of The Giants

The crew rallied round to give Vimp his well-earned rest. Lief took over and Bjorne felt good standing at the great side rudder feeling the power in his hands. A fresh breeze blew in his face and he enjoyed the sunshine streaming down from the cloudless sky. He was stunned at the height of the black cliffs along the coast. Hard, defiant rock jutted out as though they had been there, forever. And perched high up on narrow ledges, rows of seabirds guarded their eggs, or young. But above the towering cliffs circled hungry, brown skuas that harried and snatched slower victims. Skuas had young to feed, too. Ingrid stood at the helm with Bjorne. She tried to count the army of seabirds camped on the ledges of the nearest rock face.

"I give up," she shouted over the piercing cries from the cliffs. "There must be more than all the Vikings on Middle Earth! I wish I could fly free as a bird!"

It certainly seemed better than voyaging by longboat. But at that moment, a stubby-looking black and white bird crossed the bows. Ingrid marvelled at the radiant colours of its powerful, striped beak. Two small fish dangled over the lower part. A skua darted down to ambush the puffin. The helpless bird flopped dead, in the air, and its attacker flew back with it to its nest. Bjorne had been watching the spectacle.

"I'll stay human," he said, somewhat shocked. "I wouldn't want to be up on those ledges in a storm. How do the birds survive in Winter?"

The two friends remained silent for a while. Then Ingrid spotted the opening of a large inlet. It was guarded by two high, rocky headlands. The waters between the sentinels looked reasonably calm and easy to navigate.

"Is there a landing place?" she asked Bjorne. "The beaches are sandy and look easy to pull up on."

The longboat rounded the first headland.

"I can see low land behind the shore," Ingrid continued. "And grass, I think. Almost like pasture. I don't see any signs of life. No flocks or grazing animals."

Lief came to join them. His oarsmen were in a rhythm and did not need his direction. He, too, had a good feeling about the sheltered inlet.

"We've got to stop, somewhere," he said. "Our rowers need to rest. If we pitch up here we could spend a few days exploring. We can feed on fish and other sea creatures. What we now need is to find a spot where we can live off the land."

He gazed ahead.

"Not too many trees," he pointed out, glumly. "Just a few scraggy ones growing out of the wind. Following the lines of streams."

The three agreed this was the place to beach and Lief went forward to tell the crew. Bjorne turned to Ingrid. He needed to tell her what was on his mind.

"It's some time," he said, "since we saw what you might call 'joined-up' mainland. In the last two days, we've pushed farther North and passed a few strung out islands. My concern is that we've left the land of Saxons. If we push on, we might never find another island!"

Ingrid thought she understood.

"You mean we could run out of land and end up lost at sea?"

Bjorne nodded, unruly hair flying in his face.

"Winter isn't that that far away," he said. "We're way up North. But never mind the seabirds; what about us? If we don't find the right spot to settle before the icy winds blow, we'll perish. At least these islands are rocky. We can work out how to put up rough shelters."

He steered the boat between the massive headlands guarding the inlet entrance. The wind dropped.

"This'll do!"

The bay looked sheltered although the surrounding land was uninhabited. Lief and Freya stood at the mast as the boat approached the shore. Before they made their final move, they had a quiet word with Vimp. He was feeling stronger.

"We're going in to land," Lief called to the oarsmen. "Vimp's happy with this place. It looks like a safe haven."

But Lief and Vimp were in for a big shock. A huge boulder hurtled through the air and plummeted into the nearby sand. On top of the higher headland, strode an enormous figure; bearded, long-haired and wild. He towered over the inlet as the adventurers crouched in their boat. A voice of thunder echoed from the cliff top.

"Come out, Herman, you coward! It is I, Saxie, who calls. I invite you to take up my challenge."

Lief jumped up and commanded the oars.

"Pull!" he cried. "Pull with every muscle!"

Another missile sped through the air, this time hitting the water. The longboat rocked on the powerful wave created by it. It pitched up and down as the swell passed underneath. At the point where the cliffs met the sea, a noisy bubbling and boiling of water forced itself through a rocky hole. Bjorne steered away. He heard the tide fizzing and hissing in the basin that steamed like a cauldron over a fire.

"D'you hear, me, Herman?" repeated the booming voice. "You owe me half an ox!"

To the despair of the Viking crew, a third lump of rock whistled over the boat. It crashed into the cliff face across the inlet. The giant shook his fist, angrily, as a second figure appeared on the opposite headland.

"You won't get anything out of me!" the new titan roared. "I've eaten my ox, bones and all. There's nothing left for you, except the tail. You can use that to tie up your tunic!"

A deep, rumbling growl echoed from over the water. Saxie was getting angrier by the minute.

"You asked me for the loan of my boiling sea kettle," he thundered. "You promised to give me half of that ox when it was cooked. And you've gone back on your word."

He bent down, broke off an enormous chunk of earth and prepared to toss it over. Meanwhile, giant Herman wobbled precariously on his own headland. He held a massive block, ripped out of the cliff top.

"You insult me," he shouted. "Take this!"

The projectile sailed from one headland to the other and crashed in front of Saxie's gigantic feet. Part of the cliff crumbled and thundered down, dust and debris rising in the air. When the cowering Vikings looked up they saw a tidal wave heading for them.

"Stow the oars!"

Lief's command saved the day. The rowers lifted their oars seconds before the water monster lifted the longboat. The craft pitched and rolled but remained upright. High on the headlands, the giants continued their barrage of insults.

"You couldn't hit an island in front of your fat nose!"

"Pebbles don't frighten me, Beetle Legs!"

"Your ugly wife can do better than you, Frog Spawn!"

Rocks, bellows and bad language flew to and fro. The sailors had to protect themselves as chunks of cliff rained down. Vimp issued immediate orders.

"Get on that helm, Eric. We've got to get of here. Bjorne, help the rowers!"

Despite massive boulders exploding into the sea, the oarsmen rowed furiously out of the bay. The titanic row, created by Herman's broken promise, stormed on. Saxie's kettle was the boiling cauldron of sea water. Herman had used it to boil his ox but refused to hand over the promised half. The battle had raged for hundreds of years. As the longboat rowed away, Saxie and Herman stood on their headlands shaking fists and swapping insults.

It was a relief to escape to the choppier waters of the open sea. Once the excitement died down, Lief had words with Freya.

"I don't know where we're heading," he said. "We lost contact with the mainland and escaped the sea witch. We've nearly been sunk by rocks flying through the air. What next? These are crazy islands. We must find somewhere calmer to settle. No whirlpools or mad giants!"

Freya agreed.

"We'll find somewhere," she said. "Didn't you hear what the argument was about? They were going on about an ox. That can only mean one thing…"

Lief got the message. Freya was suggesting the chance of some of the islands being grazed. But which ones? If only they could find a settlement. Even if it had to be with the fierce Picts.

"One thing's certain," Freya concluded. "It can't go on like this. No-one can stay at sea, forever. How long is our search going to take?"

Under Vimp's command, the longboat headed further West. But that risked losing sight of land, altogether. If they sailed too far, they might get lost in a vast ocean. It was essential to find the mainland, once more.

The longboat ploughed on. But the crew had to be wary of tiny islands and jagged rocks on which they could founder. They entered a treacherous-looking stretch of water with racing tides and swift currents. Eric took over the tiller, with Bjorne standing by. He gazed out over the churning, white-topped waves.

"The perfect landing place doesn't exist," he told himself. He cast a glance at Astrid and the sleeping Beowulf. "Perhaps it never did!"

* * * *

CHAPTER FIFTEEN

The Mermaid's Cage

As the battered longboat struggled along the coast, the weather continued to hold. It was about the only piece of fortune the young Vikings had enjoyed since setting out. They were navigating the turbulent waters of the Western Isles. Threading their way between one island and the next meant fighting tides sweeping in from the Atlantic Ocean. The biggest problem was finding a place to land. Freya and the girls acted as look-outs. Their job was to try and detect signs of life. Just now and again, a curl of smoke rose into the sky. That had to mean human settlement. But if they tried to land, the crew had no idea how they would be welcomed. They suspected Viking longboats had prowled these islands before. If their crews had acted violently, Vimp and company feared the worst.

The girls had also been instructed to look out for dangerous rocks. Some were easy to see whilst others got covered at high tide, close to the surface. The longboat needed only about a metre of water beneath it to sail. Most of the time, it managed to stay clear of hazards. Ingrid and English Emma stood at the shattered prow of their tattered vessel and looked ahead. Strong waves beat on the rocky coast of the nearest island. And thundering spumes of spray burst into clouds before collapsing into the sea. As they passed a rocky spit projecting from the shore, they heard a new sound. A low moaning; almost musical. They had heard it before and it made Emma happy.

"Seals!" she said simply. "I love them. Their calls are so gentle. But they're very nosey. They might swim out to look at the boat."

Ingrid was a seal fan, too.

"D'you remember when they surrounded us? Staring up from the water. Those big eyes and side whiskers. They don't see many humans so they're curious. At home, our boats used to hunt them. Their blubber was used for candles and the skins kept sailors warm. Why are humans so cruel to wild creatures?"

The strange, eyrie sounds continued. It was almost like singing. From their vantage point, the girls saw the seals lolling on rocks, on the nearest island. They looked so human. Emma could hear no other sound. It was both beautiful and mesmerising as it carried across the water. For the first time in ages, she felt at peace. The singing seemed to blot out all anxieties. She relaxed to enjoy the gentle motion of the boat. What she did not realise was that the sounds were having a similar effect on her companions.

It was the same for the rowers. Even with their backs to the music, the oarsmen grew enchanted. Rowing no longer seemed to require effort. They smiled as they pulled the next stroke, drawing happily towards the seal choir. Even bold Eric relaxed into a trance at the helm. He had never heard such sweet sounds and steered the craft towards them.

Only English Emma kept her head. As the longboat drew closer to the rocks, she saw the singers were not seals. She tried to open her mouth to speak but words refused to come out. The creatures draped over the rocks looked human. But, as one slipped into the sea, she saw it possessed a scaly tail. They were close, now. Three pretty maidens smiled serenely from their rocky perches, golden ringlets of hair tumbling to their shoulders. Ingrid was right. They did possess tails. She had heard about these beings in tales her seafaring grandfather told. They were mermaids beckoning the crew to join them on their rocks. Ingrid sensed the danger and tried to call to Eric. Again, no words came as the enthralled helmsman set course for collision.

The choir of mermaids sang sweetly as the Viking longboat crunched into a jagged outcrop. It rose out of the water, timbers splitting, and rolled over. Ingrid was dragged under the surface, gulping water into her lungs. She coughed, spluttered and struck out wildly, grabbing a wooden spar torn from the boat. The tide dashed her against the rocks before sweeping her out again. Ingrid's frail body bobbed on the surf like a floundering fish.

A pair of arms wrapped gently around her waist. Half-drowned, she rolled over to find a beautiful maiden supporting her. The girl smiled, before twisting round with a flap of her tail to bear Ingrid to the depths. The Viking girl blacked out and it was several hours before she became conscious. Her head swam with confused images. When she opened her eyes, she imagined she was in in the middle of a nightmare.

"Where am I?"

Her frightened voice echoed round a damp cave. Only a trace of green-blue light penetrated. The deep rumble of tide filled the cavern. She lay on a rock bed of seaweed. Shocked and stunned, Ingrid peered into the dim light. A pretty face looked into her misty eyes.

"I don't know your name."

The mermaid hauled herself out of the water and slid next to her.

"You're one of the fortunate ones," she said. "You survived. Now, your troubles are over. You will remain with us for always. One day, you may become like we are."

Ingrid shivered in the bleak gloom. It was so hard to see even a small distance. The sea continued to thunder into the cavern.

"Your friends are here," the maid continued. "Not all, of course. We did our best to rescue but many are lost. In any case, how could we keep you all? The cavern isn't large."

She smiled sweetly.

"I'm sure we can be friends."

Ingrid's eyes were getting used to the dark. She could make out the half-human, half-fish who sat close by. The mermaid's hair fell almost her waist where it met the fishy scales of her tail. Her face and arms were pale. She smiled, serenely. Yet Ingrid suspected a coldness in her green eyes. She understood she was held a prisoner with no way out.

Cold drops of water dripped from the roof. They hit the hard floor, echoing around the walls. The young captive was aware of other people trapped close by. In the dim light, she saw prone bodies lying over the floor. One person groaned and rolled over. Another called out, feebly. Ingrid recognised the timid voice.

"Is anyone there?"

Ingrid dragged herself up onto her knees and peered into the blackness.

"Astrid, is that you?"

The mermaid edged closer. She wished to keep the two friends apart.

"Don't distress yourself. Your friends must rest."

Ingrid slumped onto her bed of damp seaweed wondering who might be sharing her ordeal. The mermaid tried to comfort her.

"No harm will befall you. Regard yourself as our guest. We will bring you news of your old world. Occasionally, we spot a boat like yours passing by. That's when we sing. Other sailors have visited this cavern before you. It's so sad. They pine for sunshine and fresh air. But they lose heart and die. We have to replace them. This is why you are here."

Ingrid could not have felt more miserable. How could she survive in this gloom? Escape was impossible with the sea roaring in at the entrance. She would be dashed to pieces on the rocky sides. Another figure stirred on a ledge, close by.

"Ingrid, it's me, Lief! I've swallowed so much water, I feel sick. How many of us are there?"

The young prisoner's heart leapt.

"I can just see you," she cried. "It's just you, me and Astrid."

She crawled across the hard rock floor and felt for Lief's chilled hand. He grasped it, weakly, and helped her sit beside him.

"It was the singing," he said. "It was so spellbinding. I tried calling to Eric but he'd been taken. Our beautiful boat broke in half. Most of the rowers drowned. We're the lucky ones."

He paused and shivered in the oppressive blackness.

"If you call this luck," he added.

The long hours passed slowly, but neither captive had much idea of the time. Mermaids slipped in and out of the cavern to view their new captives.

"We've brought you shellfish," they said. "Mussels from the rocks and cockles dug from the sand."

As time wore on, the survivors linked up. Vimp remained half-conscious, hardly knowing what was going on. English Emma lay bruised and sore whilst Eric sat huddled in a sad hump, refusing to communicate. Bjorne, too, had managed to stay alive but was distressed to discover his friend, Tharg, had drowned. To Ingrid's relief, it turned out that Freya had survived. So just the seven plus herself. All the others had perished. Lief tried to raise their low spirits after the mermaids slipped out.

"We can't stay here," he said. "I've no idea how we got here. But if there's a way in, there's a way out. The mermaids know the secret."

Lief had already worked out the escape route had to be under water.

"Bjorne and I are up for exploring," he said. "When we're on our own, we can dive and find out. It'll be dangerous when the tide floods in. But when it's at its lowest we might discover a way out."

He sounded more confident than he felt. Diving in pitch blackness was about as perilous an activity as he could think of. There was no choice. Remaining in the underwater dungeon meant death. From starvation or distress.

Although the captives could not calculate, the days outside the cavern went by. Lief worked out that the mermaids returned for longer periods, at night. During the day, they preferred to sun themselves. The person no-one could get through to was miserable Eric. He stayed in his dark corner, refusing to speak. Vimp crawled up to him.

"Why are you taking it out on yourself?" he said. "It wasn't your fault we ended up on the rocks. We were all under the mermaids' trance. No-one could resist their singing. You're not to blame."

He slipped a damp arm round Eric's shoulder. The longboat helmsman tried to speak through his tears.

"Of course it was my fault," he sobbed. "I was weak and let the music get to me. I tried to resist but my mind went blank. It's a terrible thing to lose a boat and half your crew."

Gentle Astrid joined the two boys. She felt for Eric's cold hand.

"Vimp's right. You know that. It would have happened to anyone steering."

But Astrid knew the real reason for the deep sadness at the bottom of Eric's heart.

"We know you're missing your beloved Beowulf," she whispered. "That's the bit that really hurts."

Eric's head slumped. Suddenly he let out a howl of anguish that echoed around the cavern. Astrid and Vimp held him tight. The big, brave Viking boy who had been in so many scrapes and rescues could not stand the pain of his terrible loss.

There was a sudden flurry at the water edge and two mermaids appeared with handfuls of shell fish.

"Time to eat!" they trilled merrily. "We hope you're settling in. It's lovely having company. Stay as long as you wish!"

Few of the captives found they could face another meal of uncooked seafood.

"We're just popping out to the rocks!"

The mermaids, unaware of the distress of their guests, dived deep and out of the cavern. The eight survivors moved together in a huddle to keep each other warm. Moments later, a familiar voice sounded from the water swirling below them.

"Hello, you folks! I've been searching all over. Got talking to the mermaids. You know what they're like. Chitter chatter, chitter chatter! Never stop. Bad as my wife, I can tell you."

It was the Murrough, cheerful as ever. There was a short pause whilst he dived to oxygenate his gills before popping up again.

"I've been sniffing around," he went on. "Found a secret way in. Same way out, of course. Just one problem…'

He dived again.

"You're too large to squeeze through. Need to take a look. Who's the best swimmer?"

The captives were struck dumb. Vimp recovered first as the Murrough turned and dived. He waited impatiently for his return.

"Bjorne's the strongest swimmer," he said. "He can hold his breath for ages."

Vimp could just make out Bjorne's figure crouching in the dark. The deputy helmsman was up for it.

"I'll do anything to escape, Mr Murrough. I can't get any wetter. Tell me what I have to do."

The Murrough invited Bjorne to join him but stay close. It involved a short underwater swim. After that, the Murrough explained, they would find a side cavern which led to the light. But there was a problem and that was what the Murrough wanted Bjorne to see.

Without further discussion, Bjorne slipped into the water.

"Take care," called Ingrid. "Don't take any risks!"

The Murrough advised taking a deep breath. When they emerged, Bjorne found what the merman had said was true. They were in a second, narrower cavern. He blinked in the welcome light streaming through the entrance. However, as he approached it, he saw the problem the Murrough could not solve. Thick iron bars reached down from the ceiling and beneath the water level. The spaces between were little wider than Bjorne's clenched fist. It was a cruel blow. However hard he wrenched at the bars they would not shift. Freedom and light were within his grasp yet he was still a prisoner.

"See the problem?" said the Murrough. "I can squeeze through but not even Freya or Astrid would get through. You'll have to come up with a brilliant idea!"

He took his customary dive then told Bjorne he would go away to think. Meanwhile, the Murrough desperately hoped the captives might find the answer.

"I'll pop back, later," he said. "Don't give up. I'm sure you'll think of something!"

* * * *

CHAPTER SIXTEEN

A Place To Settle?

Bjorne's return to the main cavern did not raise spirits.

"I'm sorry," he told them, "but the Murrough expected too much. He's found an escape route but it's cut off by thick iron bars. I couldn't shift them. He suggested I reported back as one of you might come up with a bright idea. But what we really need are hammers and saws. They went down with the boat. The Murrough doesn't have the strength to fetch them. He's too spindly. But give him credit. He means well."

Freya listened carefully.

"If I've got it right," she said, "we've got to break those bars. Well, we have four strong boys. You could find lumps of rock and beat them 'til they bend."

Vimp and Lief were willing to give it a go although not keen on the underwater swim. Eric sat, apart, showing no interest. His spirit was broken and he wanted to be left alone. Vimp crawled up to him and did not mince his words.

"You're not helping, Eric," he said. "No-one's a strong as you, yet you're doing nothing. What about Astrid? D'you want her kept locked up for the rest of her life?"

Vimp was close to losing his cool.

"I think you're pathetic. You've blown!"

He snorted angrily.

"Eric Bignose the brave, bold Viking? What a joke!"

It was a stupid thing to say and it dented Eric's pride. The former helmsman swung round and punched Vimp on the chin. He scrambled to his feet to do more damage. Astrid moved over in the bleak light and begged Eric to stop. She grabbed his arm just as he was about to deliver his next blow. He slipped on a strand of seaweed and fell over.

"Don't bug me!" he cried. "I'm all tensed up."

His friends backed off. Eric swallowed his pride and offered Vimp his hand.

"I'm really sorry. I blew," he said. "I'm with you. Show me the way!"

It was a great moment. The captives' spirits were lifted. With Eric on board, anything was possible. Minutes later, the three boys led by Bjorne braved the underwater channel to surface in the secret cavern. They examined the bars but were disappointed to find they refused to budge. Eric went on the search for a stray lump of rock. He staggered towards the cage and brought the rock down, hard. It shattered in pieces, making no impact on the bars. The boys took turns to try to bend the iron but the bars remained in place. Vimp called for a rest. He could not face going back to the girls with the bad news. A sudden disturbance in the water caught his eye. Illuminated by a thin beam of sunlight was the little Murrough. He was surprised to see all four boys.

"I heard the racket you're putting up," he said. "Be careful. Sound travels. We don't want those mermaids interfering. That would put an end to your escape plans."

He plunged back under for a breather but it was not long before he splashed up again.

"As I was saying. No noise or brute force. We need to think this one out!"

Eric, who had performed much of the hard work, was in no mood for lectures from a half fish.

"If you're so smart, Murrough," he challenged, "why don't you come up with the answer? You could have warned us about mermaids when we were on the boat. Even I've heard tales about their singing. Except I thought it was all rubbish."

The Murrough cocked his big fishy eye at Eric. He almost seemed to smile.

"Well," he said, "perhaps I can come up with the answer. If you get nearer to the bars, I'll show you."

The boys crowded round as the Murrough swam out.

"I'll be back!"

Vimp had no idea what he was up to. Was he 'all talk'? But it was not long before the merman re-appeared with a flourish and asked the boys to look into the light. As they did so, a dark shadow fell across the cavern. A large, hairy paw reached in, from outside, and closed round the nearest bar. Vimp noticed curved, black claws gripping the metal. A second paw grabbed the next bar. It was not long before both began to give way. Little by little, they were being pulled apart. Just enough for a slim, human body to slip through.

Eric watched in disbelief as the gap widened. Was he imagining things? A furry muzzle poked through the damage, followed by the familiar face of a very wet bear. Its little black eyes scoured the dim interior. Eric groped forward and touched the bear he knew so well. Beowulf grunted, delightedly. The other boys gathered round to bury their hands in his thick fur. It was a triumphant moment for the Murrough.

"Don't ever tell me fish have no brains," Eric said sparkily. "Get back to those girls and bring them here, right now. The mermaids may return at any time. You've not a moment to lose."

Vimp came alive and issued instructions.

"Eric, stay with Beowulf. If it's possible, make the gap wider. We might get two out at a time."

Back in the major cavern, the girls plucked up courage to face the underwater swim. When they came up for air, in the new cavern, they were stunned by the light. Astrid thought she was dreaming. Silhouetted behind the bars was the bulky figure of a brown bear. Vimp was in no mood for happy reunions.

"Look sharp!" he ordered. "Ingrid…you go first."

One after the other, the girls squeezed through to escape. Vimp chose to leave last. They were out!

"Keep down," he urged. "Crawl along that ledge covered in seaweed. Not a word from anyone."

The little Murrough swam gamely alongside, worrying about the punishment he would suffer if the mermaids discovered his treachery. The thought of facing the fearsome Mrs Murrough made him kick faster.

Eric was amazed at the size of Beowulf. The bear seemed to have grown nearly into an adult in the short time since the wrecking. It was truly mysterious. The escapers struggled on, splashing through rock pools and keeping a wary look-out. To their dismay, they stumbled across bits and pieces of the longboat. Shattered timbers lay scattered along the shoreline. Yet the party was in for a spot of luck.

"Over there!"

Bjorne drew Lief's attention to a pile of debris, washed up on the shore.

"Is that a water barrel? A couple of crates… food, maybe?"

The mermaids were not to be seen so Bjorne led the escapers to the booty. Whilst they sifted through, Vimp and Eric stood guard. The sooner they got away from the rocks, the better. Vimp noticed a winding stream running down from the hill, above.

"We'll strike inland," he ordered. "Pick up what you can and follow me."

He took the first step only to be called back by Lief.

"What should we do about the Murrough?" he asked.

Lief sensed the little merman wanted to stay with his new companions. But how would the fragile half-fishman cope out of water? He would never make it up the slope. Bjorne knew what to do.

"We left an empty barrel back on the rocks. Someone come with me. We'll half-fill it with water and drag it up between us."

Eric volunteered. With Beowulf padding after him, he helped Bjorne to dip the barrel into the sea. After all, it was the Murrough who had rescued the young voyagers. Stocked with a plentiful supply of seaweed, the merman settled down as his two slaves dragged the barrel after them. The short episode had given Lief and Vimp time to consider the next step. They had no idea of the size of the island but knew they had to explore. The sun sank in the early evening. Reaching the brow of the hill, Freya stopped everyone in their tracks.

"Look!" she hissed. "Over the next hill...smoke!"

Her pulse quickened.

"We're not alone."

The hungry escapers did not know what to think. Their spirits were still low after the shock of the shipwreck. Now they had little fight left. Bjorne and Eric plonked down the Murrough's water barrel. The others gathered round to discuss what to do. There was little choice. Stranded upon a barren island, the future seemed bleak. Yet, in their Viking hearts, they knew the only chance was to make contact. Freya took up the challenge.

"It's a risk," she said. "Massive. We must find out."

It was agreed they would reach the crest of the hill where they would make their final decision. Climbing proved tough.

The youngsters were weak with hunger, whilst Bjorne and Eric had to drag the Murrough's heavy load. Vimp was first to reach the brow and crouched in the heather. The others slid alongside and peered over the top. They looked down on a small cluster of primitive, stone dwellings. Rough, low thatches acted as roofs to keep out the rain. They were tied down by ropes, fixed to the ground by heavy stones. Small, bent figures cut slabs of brown peat from a nearby bog. Once dried, it would act as fuel to warm the huts. Hardy-looking sheep nibbled at wiry grass covering the hillside. And beyond the simple homes, other folks worked at the thin soil, digging and picking vegetables. Vimp turned to Freya and Lief.

"I suggest the three of us go down to speak to them. We're only going to perish up here on the hill. If we can make ourselves understood, these people might not be hostile."

Freya thought back to the time when she and Tharg had tried to contact alien Vikings, in her old village. They had ended up prisoners. Vimp's plan was risky.

"We'll go down as a group," she advised. "Then they'll know how many we are. We're not much of a threat!"

The scheme appealed to Lief.

"She's right. Let's face it. We don't look very fierce!"

Vimp got everyone to their feet. He agreed that the starving group hardly appeared menacing. They were a band of unarmed teenagers; lost and helpless. Nevertheless, their hearts were in their mouths as they set off.

Two sheep turned and scattered, setting off another pair. The movement caught the attention of the peat-diggers who glanced up from their work. A child sped back to the huts to raise the alarm. Moments later, dogs barked and people streamed out. Men hurried from hut to hut, or ran in from the fields. The youngsters stopped half-way down as the settlers came out, brandishing weapons. They held stout shields and lined up, ready to do battle.

"Keep going!" Vimp ordered, although doubting they were doing the right thing. "They can see we're not armed."

This was easier said than done. The men at the foot of the hill moved up. Women held their children back. One thick-set fellow strode in front of his comrades, long hair tumbling over his shoulders. He raised his sword and called out.

"He's telling us to come no further," Lief said. "What are we supposed to do?"

It was the trickiest decision Vimp ever had to make.

"We go on," he said. "Eric and Bjorne, put the Murrough's barrel down. Everybody raise their hands above their shoulders. Show these people we mean no harm."

The opposing forces moved suspiciously towards each other. Now, the hard faces of the men could be seen; stern and forbidding. As they advanced, they held the wooden shields across their chests. Their intentions were obvious. They were ready to fight.

Freya dashed forward a few paces. She did not know what language the people spoke but knew it hardly mattered.

"We are friends," she called out in her native Norse. "See! We have no weapons."

She turned and gestured towards the defenceless party.

"We come in peace!"

The leader stopped the advance of his men whilst the youngsters stayed routed to the spot. Freya, however, continued down the hillside. As the ground levelled, she broke into a run, blonde hair flying in the wind. Only paces away, the leading man dropped his sword and shield. She flung herself into his outstretched arms. A cheer went up from the men who put down their weapons before ploughing up the hill.

"Freya? Is it you?"

Chieftain Harald and his beloved daughter clung to each other for dear life. Tears of joy rolled down the Viking leader's weathered cheeks. Women gathered round, thrilled at the unexpected reunion. Then they ran up the slope to greet their long lost children. Lief's mother flung her arms round the son she thought she would never see again.. Bjorne was nearly bowled off his feet as his father cannoned into him. A wild-looking woman singled out Eric. She eyed him up and gave him a loud telling off.

"Where've you been, you naughty boy? Your father has had to do all the fishing by himself. You always were a difficult lad. Oh, I could… I could…"

She hugged her strong son and smothered him in kisses.

"Eric Bignose," she wept, "it's a good thing I love you!"

The tall, young Viking lifted his mother off her feet and swung her round.

"Sorry, mum!" he laughed. "It just seemed like a good idea at the time."

When his mother's feet touched earth again, she was horrified to find herself confronted by a large brown bear. Eric plonked her on Beowulf's back. She demanded to be put down.

"I'm not having this bear in my hut," she protested. "Whoever heard of such a thing? It would be uncivilised!"

Eric lifted her down.

"He's too good for that," he told his mother, firmly. "Beowulf will have his own hut. And if he's willing, I'll share it with him!"

Sadly, the joy for all the youngsters was not shared. Vimp soon realised his parents were not amongst the happy throng. What had happened to them? His younger brother explained.

"Mum and dad were lost at sea," he said. "In a storm. We're all orphans, Vimp, you included."

English Emma stood quietly to one side. She was the only young survivor who had no-one to greet her. Her Saxon family were back in England. Lief sensed her sadness and asked her over to meet his mother and father.

"You remember the Chieftain's slave girl, Emma?" he said. "The Saxon who was going to be sacrificed?"

He looked his parents in the eye.

"From now, you have a new daughter."

Lief's mother looked fondly at Emma took her in her arms.

"You're our family, now, Emma' she said. "Come and live with us."

Ingrid and Astrid hung onto their parents' arms. The delighted party made their way down the hillside. Soon, they reached the heart of the hamlet where other Vikings gathered round. Freya walked hand in hand with Vimp. Chieftain Harald kept with them.

"Vimp's been a brother to me," said Freya. "Far more than that. He saved my life."

Her father beamed down on them both.

"We'd be proud if you will share our humble dwelling, Vimp," he said.

He took his daughter's arm and led the way.

"Freya, there's someone you haven't seen yet. Since landing here, your mother's not been well. Go in and talk to her. You're the very best thing that could have happened. Be gentle," he urged. "Seeing you will come as a great surprise."

He turned to Vimp.

"We'll let the young lass handle this," he said. "Her mother's frail but she'll mend."

Vimp and the Chieftain strode past the grey, stone huts cowering under the hill.

"You must tell me everything, young man. From start to finish. Your friends were never far from our thinking."

Vimp understood.

"We missed you, too," he said.

The Chieftain looked at the boy, kindly.

"Maybe you taught us all a lesson. Later, we learned to respect the wishes of boys who didn't want to become warriors. Vikings have been responsible for so much slaughter, over the years. So from now, it must cease."

Vimp asked what had become of Olaf Skullcrusher, the warrior trainer the boys feared most.

"The coward's not with us," Chieftain Harald scoffed. "When the village was attacked by wild Norsemen, Olaf Skullcrusher was the first to flee. He escaped to the forest. No-one knows what became of him."

He looked grimly at Vimp.

"There are wolves in those woods."

Vimp knew. They walked on.

"I shall never forgive myself," Harald continued. "I was Chief when our village was over-run. The Norsemen meant to trade us with people, even further North. We were to be swapped as slaves for seal and bear skins."

Harald and Vimp wound slowly out of the hamlet to circle the fields providing sparse food. The Chieftain explained how a frightful storm had separated the boats of their captors. After battling with tides and winds, their own longboat foundered on rocks. They had no choice but to settle on this wild, windswept island.

"We were fortunate," Harald went on. "We stumbled upon a colony of Vikings already settled here with animals...sheep, pigs...geese. They made us welcome. We lead a hard life. In Winter, there are only a few hours of light in the day. The long nights can be very dreary. That's when we sing and tell tales around the fire."

He smiled and gazed up into the hills.

"Of course, this will never be like our old homeland. But we're alive and free. Home is what you make of it."

Vimp did his best to fill in the Chieftain on the adventures he and his friends had experienced. He told him of the return to the old village where they discovered it occupied by hostile warriors. And the terrible disappointment of not finding their families.

"There's a lot to catch up on," Harald agreed as they approached the huts. "I don't think we'll be short for time. You and your pals can entertain us on those Winter evenings."

A small crowd had formed at the centre of the settlement. Young children buzzed with excitement at the sight of the little Murrough splashing in his water butt. They were equally enchanted, by the large brown bear that kept strict guard on his friend. Already, preparations for celebrations were underway. Men gathered wood to light a fire and roast two sheep for the feast. And women prepared chopped vegetables for the steaming cauldron. Eric drew Vimp on one side.

"Having a fire's a great idea," he said. "It's the best thing we've seen for ages. But is it sensible? There's not much wood about. They're even using stuff from the boats that ran onto the rocks."

Vimp did not see what his great friend was getting at.

"Tomorrow morning," Eric told him, "the bear and I will search the shore for timbers. We might even find the odd box of tools washed up. I reckon we owe it to these folks to build a boat before they burn all their wood! Then we can explore the local islands and maybe sail across to the mainland."

Setting out on another adventure was the last thing in Vimp's mind. What he now wanted to do was settle and learn about farming.

"The sea's in my blood," Eric went on. "I can't help it. Whatever it throws at me, I'll be out there battling against it. It's what I'm meant to do!"

Vimp slipped an arm round the proud Viking's shoulders.

"We'll see what Astrid has to say about that," he grinned. "Although I don't suppose even she could stop you."

Eric burst out laughing.

"Exactly! And when I finish my first boat I'll name it 'Beowulf.'

The brave voyagers enjoyed that night's celebration around the fire. They told their tales like good Vikings. Except, in their case, they were all true! Next morning, bear and master set out for the beach. Eric tugged a barrel of sea water behind him. At a suitable rock pool, he lifted out the Murrough.

"This one's perfect, Mr Murrough' he told the small merman. "We'll watch out for the tide so you don't get swept away. And when we've finished we'll carry you back to the huts."

The merman dived towards the nearest strand of olive seaweed to find his breakfast. As Eric searched the shore for washed-up timbers, his bear snuffled noisily around for shellfish. But Beowulf's black eyes kept a close watch on the sea. He was ready to act if a bad-tempered mermaid turned up, demanding her husband's return. One quick snap of the bear's jaws would be sufficient warning to drive the unpleasant creature away!

* * * *

EPILOGUE

Many years later, a small party of settler Vikings climbed the hill. At the crest, some of the older children raced over to two stacks of rocks. These had been erected by the villagers, one higher than the other. Freya cradled her new baby in her arms and watched her older daughter run round the back of the smaller pile. Her husband looked on. Vimp was the new Chieftain of the community. Next to him, Lief and Emma linked arms. A toddler perched on Lief's shoulders.

"Be careful, Asvald," Emma called as one of the children tumbled over.

He scrambled to his feet with a cheeky grin. Lief smiled at Bjorne and Ingrid who stood close by. Only Astrid lacked a strong man by her side. She gripped the hand of a sturdy, eight year-old boy.

"You see the larger stack?" she said. "We built that to honour your father. It's from him you take your name. But Big Eric's body doesn't lie beneath it."

She gazed thoughtfully out to sea.

"It was never found."

Tall and serious for his age, the boy glanced up.

"I'm proud of my daddy," he said. "People say he was brave. He rescued sailors stranded in a storm. Then he swam out to the wreck a second time.

The boy's expression clouded.

"He was swept away."

Astrid slipped her arm around the child and walked over to the smaller mound.

"Under that one is buried Beowulf, your father's bear. He lost the will to live after his master failed to return. Now, their memorials lie side by side forever."

She looked over the bay and pointed to an elegant longboat beached on the shore. The man she adored had been its designer and builder.

"D'you see the prow, Young Eric?" said Astrid. "And the carved figure of a handsome bear?"

The boy nodded, gravely.

A shadow flitted briefly across the gathering. Astrid turned her beautiful face to the sky where, high in the clouds, circled a mighty sea eagle. The bird spread its broad wings and glided down, sweeping low over the watchers' heads.

Astrid protected her eyes as the bird flew back towards the sun. She smiled, raised an arm and saluted.

She needed no telling. She knew.

ABOUT THE AUTHOR

Peter Ward worked nearly 20 years writing, script-commissioning and directing for BBC Radio Four and Schools Broadcasting. He became a Chief Producer and Editor with BBC Education originating scripts on the natural world, biotechnology, science, health, sport, computer applications and teenage issues. A ground-breaking Primary Schools series *Maths - with a Story!* led to two suites of early educational software.

A part-time and strictly fair weather sailor, Peter helms a small dinghy on Bewl reservoir in SE England. He freely admits he would make a hopeless, indeed grossly inadequate, Viking adventurer!

After taking an Honours Science degree at the University of London, Peter taught for five years in Inner London Secondary Comprehensive Schools. And later, nine enjoyable years at a State Primary School. This is where he developed his taste for children's literature and poetry. At this time, he grew concerned about the problem of getting boys to read fiction. The Viking Trilogy attempts to tackle this problem, head on-without neglecting the girls!

Currently, the author sings in three local choirs challenging a range of music from Monteverdi to Broadway. At the time of writing, a young people's Musical based on his first book published by Trafford *Vimp the Viking's Epic Voyage* is under development.

Father of two daughters, the author dedicates his **Viking Trilogy** to young grandson, Jack, who patiently acts as Consultant to problems created by the complexities and frustrations of home computers.

Living in a small, rural village in East Sussex with Patterdale Terrier Pickle, Peter's next writing project will be to place his much loved dog at the heart of a new children's adventure story with a scientific theme.

ALSO BY PETER WARD

The Adventures of Charles Darwin
Cambridge University Press
Re-issued in paperback 2009
(Fully illustrated; age range 9-11)
ISBN: 978-0-521-31074-1

'Children's writing at its best' **Nature Magazine**
'An excellent introduction to young readers' **Times Literary Supplement**
'If Darwin sounds a bit heavy, think again' **The Sun, Australia**
'A minor classic' **Junior Librarian**

Vimp the Viking's Epic Voyage
Trafford 2008
(Fully illustrated; age range 9-12)
ISBN: 978-1-4251-4253-7
Defiant youngsters who refuse to become warrior raiders escape by longboat to take on the Gods at sea, Viking pirates and the menacing Serpent of the World. Guided by dolphins over the North Sea, their troubles only increase once they land in Anglo-Saxon England. They hope to settle, peacefully, but the locals are in no mood to welcome would be immigrants they perceive as hostile invaders. Things get even uglier when the young Vikings' angry parents turn up in a raider boat!

Freya and the Fenris-Wolf
Trafford 2010
(Fully illustrated; age range 9- 12)
ISBN: 978-1-4269-2510-8
Heroine Freya is punished by the Viking Gods for using her mysterious powers on Earth. Banished by the Court of Odin to feed the monstrous and legendary Fenris-Wolf, Freya's only chance of survival is to be rescued by Vimp and company. Aided by wild wolves of the forest, the story reaches a stunning climax with a Viking funeral at sea. English history is interwoven with Viking mythology when the Benedictine Abbey at Lindisfarne, Northumbria, is raided by plundering Norsemen. One of the young heroes rescues the Lindisfarne Gospels (now on display in The British Library, London.)

Printed in the United States
By Bookmasters